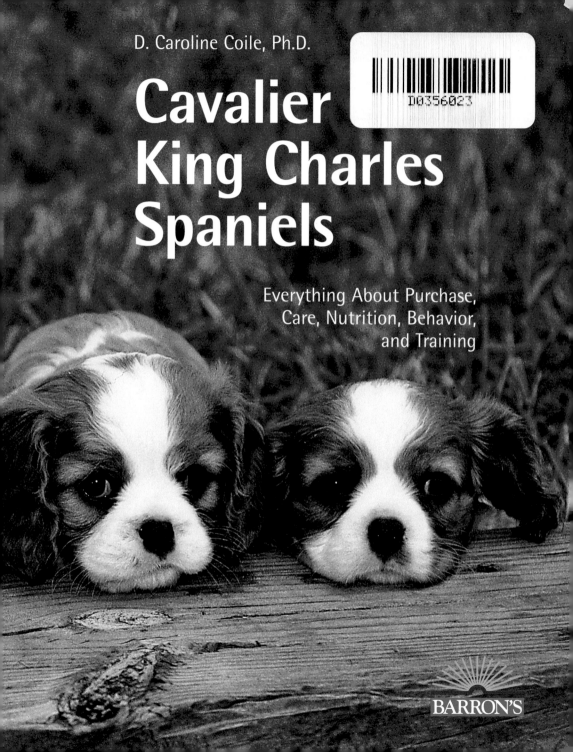

D. Caroline Coile, Ph.D.

Cavalier King Charles Spaniels

Everything About Purchase, Care, Nutrition, Behavior, and Training

BARRON'S

KING OF HEARTS

Among the many roles the dog has played throughout history, none has proved more valuable than that of companion. And few breeds have proved more companionable than the Cavalier King Charles Spaniel.

If the eyes are the window to the soul, the Cavalier King Charles Spaniel has the kindest soul in dogdom. To peer into the eyes of your Cavalier is to enjoy a vision of utter devotion and to fall completely under his spell. Those eyes have been working their magic on generations of some of the most powerful people in history. These kings may have ruled countries, but these spaniels ruled kings. Now Cavaliers are taking over families around the world.

The Cavalier's uncanny companionship capabilities stem from its remote spaniel roots, dogs that were bred to hunt in partnership with their masters. Exactly when and how the hunting spaniel became the toy spaniel has been lost in antiquity. The breeding of small dogs was perfected in the ancient Orient, and the European toy spaniels were probably the result of breeding smaller spaniels to Oriental toy breeds such as the Japanese Chin and perhaps the Tibetan Spaniel—breeds that in turn could trace their own roots to the Maltese.

The Lap of Luxury

The lapdogs of Tudor England were every bit as vital to human comfort and health as were the glorified hunting dogs of the day. Lapdogs attracted fleas from their owners' bodies, thus lessening the human diseases and discomfort spread by these scourges. The dog's high body temperature also proved an asset in the lapdog's role as lap and foot warmer on cold wintry evenings at home or on long coach rides. Dogs were even welcomed into beds as foot warmers and heating pads. A warm dog placed on an aching joint or stomach could often help alleviate pain. In fact, lapdogs were sometimes credited with curing disease by extracting their owner's illness and taking it into their own bodies. While this is sheer myth, it's now accepted that dogs can improve the health of their owners just by cuddling and comforting. And one thing was as accepted in days of old as in modern times: these "comforter spaniels" did more than warm laps—they warmed hearts.

Several lapdog types vied for preeminence, but the toy spaniels had the advantage of appealing to every member of the family. The men of the manor might coax the little spaniels out of their ladies' laps for a foray in the field to hunt small game, such as rabbits or wood-cock. The children found willing playmates in the little dogs. And the esthetic appeal of these dogs was evident to all. The little dogs thus served their people as hunters, companions, foot warmers, flea catchers, adornments, jesters, and confidants. Many breeds have tried to live up to such duties, but few as successfully as the little comforter spaniels.

The Dog Who Would Be King

The comforter spaniels wasted no time in weaving their way into every facet of their people's lives. These dogs became inseparable companions to the nobility, as evidenced by their inclusion in so many royal portraits. Few breeds have had their history documented in such royal fashion, painted by the most esteemed artists of their time. Whether cavort-ing underfoot, sitting majestically alongside, or lying comfortingly in a lap, the dogs of these fifteenth-century paintings look uncannily like the Cavaliers of today.

The comforter spaniels were a favorite of royalty throughout Europe. Mary Queen of Scots spent her youth in France, and was prob-ably introduced to the spaniels there. She in turn has been credited with introducing the lit-tle dogs to Scotland and England. When, in 1587, she was led to the gallows, her faithful black and white toy spaniel refused to leave her side. It was later removed from beneath her skirts after her beheading.

England quickly became the adopted home-land for the toy spaniels, in great part because of the dedication of King Charles I. But like that of their royal owners, the fates of the royal spaniels were forever intertwined with their tumultuous times. On the same day that King Charles I was executed at the demand of Oliver Cromwell, Cromwell's men took the king's con-stant companion spaniel, Rogue, to publicly exhibit as a trophy.

By far the most credit for the unrivaled suc-cess of the toy spaniel can be attributed to King Charles II, who regained his father's throne and ruled England from 1660 to 1685. King Charles was an unabashed aficionado of the little dogs, always having several in his company. In fact, the king was so preoccupied with his dogs that he was sometimes accused of ignoring concerns of the kingdom. One royal edict he did find time to make was that no toy spaniel could ever be denied entrance into any public building, includ-ing Parliament. It was not unusual for a dam with a litter of puppies to be found in the king's bedchambers, and a dozen of his devoted spaniels comforted him on his deathbed. So much did the little dogs come to be identified with the king that they eventually came to be called "King Charles Spaniels."

After his death, King Charles's brother, James II, took over as both king and patron of the King Charles Spaniel. His reign lasted only a few years before he was exiled to France and William III took his place as king, but not as

As its name implies, the Cavalier comes from spaniel roots.

King Charles Spaniel advocate. The new ruler favored Pugs, and so the Pug usurped the toy spaniel as official royal dog.

But the Pug could not completely take over as the dog of the nobility. Through his association with King James, the Duke of Marlborough had become completely infatuated with the little spaniels. The duke bred mostly red and white King Charles Spaniels, which became known as Marlborough or Blenheim (pronounced "blennim") Spaniels. Supposedly, while the duke was away fighting in the battle of Blenheim, his wife was at home worrying about her husband and soothing a whelping bitch. The distraught duchess comforted both herself and the prospective mother by repeatedly pressing the bitch's forehead with her thumb. When news came that the battle had been won, the puppies were born, and all bore a red "thumbmark" in the middle of

their foreheads, said to have resulted from pressing the dam's forehead! Of course, such markings are due to genes, but at the time it was a popular explanation. The name Blenheim was applied to the red and white dogs with the characteristic "Blenheim spot." Generations of Dukes of Marlborough continued to breed their Blenheim strain until the early 1900s.

King Charles Spaniels rivaled the Pug as the perennial favorite of aristocracy throughout the centuries. Queen Victoria was known for her affection for dogs of many breeds, but her particular favorite was a tricolor toy spaniel named Dash. Upon his death, his epitaph read "His attachment was without selfishness, his playfulness without malice, his fidelity without deceit."

Despite competition from the Pug, the King Charles Spaniel continued to grace the homes and cavort in the gardens of the wealthier fam-

The dark spot on the top of some Cavaliers' heads is called the Blenheim spot, or sometimes, lozenge.

ilies just as they had done for generations. But although they still displayed the typical gay, fearless, and loving temperaments that had so long endeared them to their families, their appearance was slowly changing.

Winners by a Nose

During King Charles's time, the toy spaniels had fairly long muzzles, flat skulls, and high-set ears, but by the late nineteenth century dogs with shorter muzzles, domed skulls, and low-set ears were the preferred and prevalent type. Around this same time dog showing was emerging as a pastime of the wealthy, and judging guidelines, or breed standards, were drawn up describing the ideal for each breed.

The standard for the King Charles Spaniel required a domed skull and pushed-in nose. Those dogs not meeting these criteria did not win in the show ring, and thus were not sought as breeding stock. By the early twentieth century, few dogs remained that resembled the dog so popular in earlier times.

The king's spaniel was in peril, and it took a gallant knight to rescue it. That gallant knight was a wealthy American named Roswell Eldridge, who had become enthralled by the pointy nosed spaniels pictured in the old royal paintings. So enamored was he that he traveled to England in 1926 to obtain a breeding pair for himself, but was sorely disappointed to find not a single such dog at any show. Mr. Eldridge then astounded the dog world by offering a

	Cavalier	**English Toy (King Charles)**
Weight	13–18 pounds (6–8 kg)	9–12 pounds (4–5.5 kg)
Muzzle length	medium	short
Skull	flat	domed
Ear set	high	low
Tail	undocked or docked long	docked short
Colors		
red, white	Blenheim	Blenheim
black, tan, white	tricolor	Prince Charles
red	ruby	ruby
black, tan	black and tan	King Charles

dog show class prize of 25 pounds ($125) each for best male and female "Blenheim Spaniels of the Old Type, as shown in pictures of Charles II's time, long face, no stop, flat skull, not inclined to be domed, with spot in the center of skull." Most breeders who had been striving to produce only round-headed dogs were appalled, but nonetheless several entered their "worst" (that is, longest-nosed) in the competition, and a few deliberately bred these dogs together. Roswell Eldridge died without ever finding the dog of his dreams, but could scarcely have imagined the course of events his challenge would elicit. The seed he sowed fired the imagination of several breeders, who embraced the vision of recreating the original royal spaniels.

In 1928 the first Cavalier club was formed, the first standard (modeled after a dog named Ann's Son) was written, and the English Kennel Club recognized the new type as King Charles Spaniels, Cavalier type. The name Cavalier was in homage to the political group that restored Charles II to the throne after the death of Oliver Cromwell. The name seems particularly

fitting to denote these dogs who were now being restored to their place of royalty.

Within a few years long-nosed Cavaliers were gracing the show rings as well as fine homes, although their numbers were still limited. With World War II came a devastating setback, as most of the breeding stock had to be destroyed because of hardship. Eventually, six dogs came to be the foundation from whom all modern Cavaliers descend. Their numbers and quality gradually increased, and the Cavalier was granted status in 1945 as a separate breed, the Cavalier King Charles Spaniel.

The Cavalier Versus the English Toy Spaniel

The Cavalier King Charles Spaniel and the English Toy Spaniel are constantly confused with one another. To further complicate matters, in England the English Toy Spaniel is known as the King Charles Spaniel and in the United States, one of its color varieties is known as King Charles. The two breeds resemble one another and, until the last 100 years, shared the same history and came from the same stock. The breeds come in the same four colors, but we call two of the colors by different names. The English Toy Spaniel is divided into two color varieties, the solid body colors (ruby and King Charles) and the broken colors (Blenheim and Prince Charles). The Cavalier does not separate the breed into varieties (see comparisons table on page 9).

Haute Dogs

Despite acceptance by the Kennel Club, popularity of the Cavalier rose slowly—that is, until 1973. One of the largest and most prestigious dog shows in the world is England's Crufts Dog Show. In 1973 a Cavalier named Alansmere Aquarius bested thousands of other dogs to emerge as the Best in Show at Crufts, thrusting the Cavalier into the limelight. No longer was the Cavalier the closely guarded secret of the wealthy; the little dogs with the teddy bear eyes were suddenly the darling of everybody. This was the break the breed had been waiting for, but it was not without its downside. Now there was a ready market prepared to pay top dollar for an irresistible puppy. Unfortunately, there were unscrupulous breeders ready to cash in, producing as many puppies as possible without concern for quality. Those puppies in turn were bred by their naive owners, who never realized their dogs were not up to snuff. As supply exceeded demand, prices dropped, and those who were never really in love with the breed except for its money-making potential deserted them for the next fad breed. Today the Cavalier is the most popular toy breed in England; in fact, it is one of the most popular of all breeds there. Most breeds that have achieved such popularity are rife with hereditary problems due to

uneducated or uncaring breeders. The Cavalier has sidestepped this destiny to some degree, but still has suffered from popularity.

The Controversy on the Continent

Meanwhile, the situation was very different in the United States. For Americans, lacking the constant reminders of royal heritage and oblivious to the existence of the Crufts Dog Show and its supreme victor, the Cavalier remained an anonymous face. Yet early paintings suggest that Cavaliers had made their way to the New World in Colonial times, and there was steady documented importation to America from England from 1946 on. A group of enthusiasts formed the Cavalier King Charles Spaniel Club, USA (CKCSC, USA) in 1954. The club sought recognition for the breed from the American Kennel Club (AKC), and in 1961 the AKC accepted the Cavalier into its miscellaneous class, a sort of staging area for new breeds. Still, too few Cavaliers existed in America to warrant official breed status, so the CKCSC, USA held its own shows and awarded its own championships while awaiting an increase in the breed population. The breed grew so much that the club's specialty shows attracted entries of as many as 300 Cavaliers. Official AKC recognition seemed imminent, and the invitation finally came in 1993.

Few clubs can claim the success that the CKCSC, USA has achieved, both in terms of numbers of members and service to the breed. The club maintains complete records of all Cavalier pedigrees, litters, and registered dogs. Members must abide by a strict code of ethics, which governs (among other topics) the age and num-

ber of times a dog can be bred, and the criteria for receiving full recognition. AKC recognition would mean giving the duties of registration to the AKC, thus giving up the club's quality control guidelines. These guidelines had helped keep the breed out of the hands of unscrupulous breeders, who would have found it nearly impossible to register their stock, and thus would have had difficulty selling inferior puppies. In addition, without the catch phrase "AKC registered," the puppy market would not be strong, further discouraging careless or profit-motivated breeding. Many members of the CKCSC, USA feared that AKC recognition would propel the Cavalier into the popular limelight and result in a repeat of the situation that had ultimately hurt the breed in England.

Thus, when the invitation came, it was not met with universal glee. The CKCSC, USA polled its members, who voted against accepting the AKC's invitation. While all members wanted the best for their beloved breed, they disagreed about the best way to serve it.

Some members, however, feared that if the AKC did not recognize the CKCSC, USA as the parent club for the breed, it might recognize a parent club formed of less experienced and less devoted fanciers. In self-defense they formed the American Cavalier King Charles Spaniel Club (ACKCSC) and offered themselves as the official parent club to the AKC. The AKC then officially welcomed the Cavalier into its toy group on January 1, 1996.

The Cavalier was an instant success in the show ring, quickly winning the admiration of judges and the hearts of spectators. Forewarned by the fate of their cousins in England, Cavalier fanciers are careful to promote their breed cautiously and place them only with the greatest care lest they fall into unscrupulous hands. Anyone trying to obtain a Cavalier from an ethical breeder must be prepared to be given the third degree. Nonetheless, by 2006 the Cavalier had advanced to the 27th most popular AKC breed.

The Cavalier continues to appeal to the upper crust of society throughout Europe and America. But more and more, the little spaniel with the royal cape and pauper eyes can be found transforming humble homes into Cavalier castles and any lap into the lap of luxury.

TO CAV OR CAV NOT . . .

*What would your ideal companion dog
be like? Would it eagerly join you on
a jaunt afield, bounding ahead but
taking care never to wander too far?
Would it be just as content to spend
a rainy day snuggling in your arms
as you both loll in front of a roaring
fire? Would it follow your directions
with tail awag, ever eager for your
next idea? Would it be a gentle and
trustworthy special friend for a child,
yet sound the alarm to a stranger's presence?
Then meet the Cavalier King Charles Spaniel.*

A Cavalier Attitude

How can one breed be so nearly the perfect
canine companion? Because it was bred to be.
The Cav's hunting spaniel heritage infused it
with a basic sense of adventure and outdoor
hardiness. The Cavalier King Charles Spaniel is
at heart a sporting dog, and is delighted at the
chance to get back to its roots, never missing
an opportunity to launch itself into a lake or
beat the bushes for birds.

Though the Cavalier does have a wild side, it
is tamed by an even stronger desire to please its
human partner. Because a working spaniel must
heed the hunter's directions, those early spaniels
that ran amok in the field were not used to
create the next generation of hunters, with the
result that today's Cavalier has behind it generation after generation of dogs that were eager
to comply with their masters' wishes.

No doubt the Cavalier's easy trainability
enabled it to worm its way into its master's—
and mistress's—hearts and hearths. Once there,
those dogs that particularly enjoyed staying by
the side or in the lap of their owners were
especially prized. Dogs that were always underfoot had to be trustworthy with children, and,
of course, no one could have just one Cavalier,
so the little spaniels had to also get along
with each other. Selection for these traits—
obedience, sociability, and tractability—
combined with the spaniel's innate joie de vivre
and quest for adventure—created a dog that

was the ideal companion. These very traits are the hallmark of today's Cavaliers.

Still, there are other breeds that are both obedient and fun-loving. What makes the Cavalier King Charles Spaniel so special?

Cavalier Considerations

Trainability: There are breeds that are faster to learn and faster to respond than the Cavalier. In fact, a popular book ranks the Cavalier near the middle (72 out of 133) of breeds compared for obedience and working intelligence. But you don't necessarily want your dog to rank at the top of this list. The Cavalier is too calm and low key to be a hop-to-it obedience whiz dog. It was bred to be a house companion and, as such, doesn't have the excessive activity and energy level required to excel in working obedience tests.

Size: Called the king-sized toy, the Cavalier is the largest breed in the toy group, and in some ways combines the best of both small- and medium-size dogs. The average Cavalier is 12–13 inches (30–33 cm) at the shoulder and weighs 13–18 pounds (6–8 kg). Small dogs are more economical to feed, house, and even take traveling. Small enough to tuck under your arm, yet large enough to trot alongside, the Cav's size makes it an ideal companion whether on a trip to town or cross-country. At home, the Cavalier is just the right size for cuddling, yet large enough to jump on and off your sofa or bed (if you let it) by itself, something that can be difficult or dangerous for tiny dogs.

Exercise: The Cavalier's size makes it at home in either an apartment or house, but its sporting heritage does make it necessary for it to get outdoors and run off excess energy at least once a day. Still, the Cavalier is too small to be a jogging companion for a marathon runner. And despite the Cav's friendly nature, owners must be cautioned that not all dogs are so friendly in turn, and the Cavalier is virtually defenseless against bigger dogs. As such, it should never be taken to run off-lead in areas where large dogs are also running free. In fact, the Cavalier should never be let off-lead except in the safest of places, because the Cavalier is too easily tempted by the smallest diversion. Even a fluttering butterfly can lure a cavorting Cavalier into the path of traffic.

Children: Rough children, too, can pose a danger to a small dog, especially a tolerant one. The Cavalier is extremely gentle, but every dog has its limit. Your Cav should not be pushed to the point of defending itself; it is the parent's duty to oversee any child playing with a Cav, because the Cavalier is too small for rough-and-tumble play or careless handling.

Protection: What a joke! The Cavalier's bark is indeed worse than its bite. It will welcome burglars with great gusto, with wagging tail and soaring spirit. Although some may find a barking Cavalier to be intimidating, in truth the Cavalier is not a particularly effective protection dog.

Barking: Most Cavaliers are laid back and quiet, but a few find barking to be a fascinating pastime—to the point of driving their people crazy! Some people believe that this barking tendency tends to run in lines. Overall, however, Cavaliers are content to bark a few times and then quiet down fairly quickly.

Companionship: Cavaliers take the label of "best friend" seriously. If you want a shadow to follow you everywhere, a dog that's always underfoot or in your lap, if you never want to go to the bathroom alone again—then this dog's for you. If you don't mind public displays of affection, once again, the Cavalier is your dog. Most people find these traits endearing, but some people prefer a slightly less depend-

ent or demonstrative dog, and may even accuse the Cav of being needy or clingy. Cavaliers aren't needy, except in the sense that they do need attention and companionship. If you prefer your alone time, if you don't like puppy dog eyes watching you expectantly, or if you plan to keep your dog in the yard or separated from the family, this is *not* the dog for you.

Because of their social butterfly tendencies, Cavaliers can become very anxious when left alone. Some become so anxious that they suffer from separation distress (see pages 34–35).

Other pets: Cavaliers get along well with other dogs and household pets, and in fact, most breeders feel Cavaliers do better in house-

Cavaliers make perfect companions for considerate children.

Cavaliers and cats can be best friends.

holds with at least one other pet. They especially enjoy other Cavaliers, but have no problem living with larger or smaller dogs—and even cats. They do still retain some hunting instincts, however, so common sense should rule when combining them with birds or rodents.

House-training: Toy dogs are notorious for being difficult to house-train. Cavaliers are far easier than most toy dogs in this respect, but some can still be slightly more challenging than most large-breed dogs. Part of this may stem from bad habits formed early in life. Whatever surface dogs use as their potty area when they are seven to nine weeks old is the surface they tend to prefer throughout life. And many toy dogs, especially those from pet shops, are raised indoors without a chance to learn about grass potties. It's also easy to miss or ignore accidents from tiny puppies, and also easy to have pity and decide that the grass really is too wet to

expect poor baby to go outside. Many Cavs learn that they can simply refuse to potty outdoors when the weather is not to their liking!

Some male Cavaliers, even neutered ones at times, are prone to lifting their leg to mark inside, and even some females have a tendency to mark in places you really won't appreciate—such as on your bed! Some owners have their dogs, especially the bad boys, wear pee-pads, but with some extra work, most Cavaliers can be house-trained.

Health: Like any breed, the Cavalier has its own set of hereditary health problems, in the Cav's case including heart problems, hip dysplasia, knee problems, eye problems, and some neurological disorders. This doesn't mean every Cavalier is doomed to succumb to one of these problems. If they were, there wouldn't be the great numbers of healthy Cavaliers romping about.

Good Cavalier breeders are extremely proactive and open about possible problems, more so than in most breeds. While it's true that a Cavalier with heart problems may live only seven to ten years, an otherwise healthy Cavalier can expect to live into its teens. That's one reason, however, to insist on health testing of your prospective puppy's parents before you buy. There are no guarantees in life when it comes to health, but you can hedge your bets by being a careful consumer.

Grooming: The Cavalier is blessed with the best of all worlds when it comes to its eye-catching coat. It is long enough to be luxuriously soft when cuddling, yet not so thick that constant grooming is required. As an added bonus, the Cav's coat comes in a variety of colors.

Grooming the Cavalier will require a couple of short weekly sessions, consisting of brushing or combing the longer hair while paying special

Color Me Cavalier

Coat color genetics are relatively simple for the Cavalier. A dog can either be red or black and tan, and solid or parti-colored. Think of the parti-color as a solid-colored dog that has had white paint splashed over him; under that white is still the same red or black and tan base color. Blenheim is simply the parti-color version of ruby (red). Tricolor is simply the parti-colored version of black and tan.

The gene for solid color (**S**) is dominant to that for parti-color (**s^p**). Thus, a dog with the combination **SS** or **Ss^p** will be solid colored, and a dog with the pair **ss** will be parti-colored.

Genes at two other locations determine whether the dog will have a black and tan base or a red base. The black and tan color is one of several choices at the **A**, or agouti, locus, but all Cavaliers have the black and tan gene, **a^t**, so it's really the genes at the **E**, or extension, locus that decide whether that black and tan will be expressed or not. The dominant **E** allele allows full expression; the recessive **e** restricts the expression of melanin, causing the black and tan to simply be red all over. A Cavalier that is **EE** or **Ee** will be black and tan; one that is **ee** will be red.

The four colors can have the following gene combinations:

✔ Blenheim (red **ee** plus parti-colored **s^{p}s^p**). The only possible gene combination is **ees^{p}s^p**.

✔ Ruby (red **ee** plus solid **SS** or **s^p**). Possible combinations are **eeSS** or **eeSs^p**.

✔ Tricolor (black and tan **EE** or **Ee** plus parti-colored **s^{p}s^p**). Possible combinations are **EEs^{p}s^p** or **EESs^p**.

✔ Black and Tan (black and tan **EE** or **Ee** plus solid **SS** or **Ss^p**). Possible combinations are **EESS**, **EESs^p**, **EeSS**, or **EeSs^p**.

attention to areas that tend to mat. Bathing is only rarely needed. The Cavalier sheds neither more nor less than most other breeds.

Royal Colors

The Cavalier comes in two different colors (black and tan, or red), and two different patterns (solid, or broken with white) for a total of four different color varieties:

Ruby: a solid rich tan or red, also described as chestnut.

Black and tan: distributed as the black and tan coloration of the Doberman Pinscher.

Blenheim: rich tan or red broken up by large white areas. The color extends over both eyes and ears, with a large blaze covering the muzzle and extending between the eyes. A small colored spot in the middle of the blaze near the back of the skull is commonly seen and desirable.

Tricolor: the black and tan pattern broken up by white in the same basic pattern as that seen in the Blenheim.

Each color has its own appeal, although the Blenheim is undeniably the most popular. Many owners of Cavaliers eventually find that they must have one of each!

Choosing Your Cavalier Companion

Now that you've chosen the Cavalier as your breed, it's time to take the same care in choosing your own special Cavalier. While it's true you could find a Cav in the newspaper, a pet store, or on the Internet with little effort, why would you consider choosing a family member with so little care? It's worth the effort to find a Cavalier that embodies the best this breed has

to offer. Remember the traits that attracted you to the Cavalier King Charles Spaniel: its looks and its personality. Remember also the all-important trait of good health.

Looks

You want your Cavalier to look like a Cavalier, so make sure the parents have at least the essence of Cavalier appearance: melt-your-heart expression, moderate-sized bone, and silky hair in vibrant colors. If you simply want a Cavalier as a companion, you need not concern yourself with the finer points of conformation. If you have aspirations of entering the show ring, you'll need to study the standard (pages 81–84), visit dog shows, and talk to breeders. You'll want to make sure your Cavalier show-dog-to-be has a champion-studded pedigree, with at least one parent holding the title of Champion.

Personality

It's hard to find a Cavalier with a poor personality, but why take chances? Although most uncommon, Cavaliers can be shy or aggressive. Try to meet both parents to make sure they have the sort of temperament you want in your Cavalier. The typical Cavalier is outgoing, vivacious, and loving. If you dream of trying obedience competition with your Cavalier, you can hedge your bet by getting one from a family of dogs that have proven their obedience aptitude by earning obedience titles (see page 85).

Health

Your best indicator of your prospective Cavalier's health is the health of not just his parents, but his aunts, uncles, grandparents, and any other family members. How long did they live? What did they die of? What sort of health

The Cavalier at a Glance

Energy level:	☐☐☐
Exercise requirements:	☐☐☐
Playfulness:	☐☐☐☐
Affection level:	☐☐☐☐☐
Friendliness toward dogs:	☐☐☐☐☐
Friendliness toward other pets:	☐☐☐☐☐
Friendliness toward strangers:	☐☐☐☐☐
Ease of training:	☐☐☐☐
Ease of house-training:	☐☐☐
Independence:	☐
Watchdog ability:	☐☐☐
Protection ability:	☐☐☐
Lap sitting ability:	☐☐☐☐☐
Grooming requirements:	☐☐☐
Cold tolerance:	☐☐☐
Heat tolerance:	☐☐
Lifespan:	☐☐☐

screening tests did they have? What health problems did they have? Did they require medical or surgical treatment to live comfortably?

Cavaliers have some serious hereditary health problems that can lead to a shortened lifespan or to reduced quality of life. Foremost among these are a heart problem called mitral valve disease, two different neurological problems (syringomyelia and episodic falling), knee and hip problems, and some eye problems. It is vital that you buy from a breeder who follows guidelines to avoid these diseases. For information about these diseases, see pages 68–71.

Unfortunately, even the worst breeder will claim they are ethical and that their dogs are health tested. Some naïve breeders believe that health testing means the puppies have been wormed. But Cavalier health testing entails a series of tests for the presence of several different hereditary diseases. Because these test results are meaningless in some cases if the dog is below a certain minimum age, you need to find out the following from the breeder:

✔ The registered names and the birthdates of both parents.

✔ The exact tests the dogs have had, when they had them, what the results were, and what documentation is available.

Given this information, you can confirm many of the tests results online through the Orthopedic Foundation for Animals (*www.offa.org*), the Canine Health Information Center (*www.caninehealthinfo.org*), and the Canine Eye Registry (*www.vmdb.org/inquiry.html*). Of course, after going through the expense and effort of testing, a good breeder should be happy to give you this information and documentation. Good breeders test the parents of any litter they breed for the following conditions:

Mitral valve disease (MVD): MVD is the leading cause of premature (non-accidental) death in Cavaliers. Over half of Cavaliers over age five years have MVD murmurs. Veterinary cardiologists and geneticists advocate the following protocol in order to both lessen the frequency of MVD and increase the age at which it occurs:

✔ Every breeding Cavalier King Charles Spaniel should be examined annually by a board certified veterinary cardiologist.

✔ No Cavalier that has been diagnosed with an MVD murmur under the age of five years should be bred.

✔ No Cavalier should be bred before $2^{1/2}$ years of age.

✔ No Cavalier under the age of five years should be bred, unless its parents' hearts were free of MVD murmurs by age five years.

The dates of the examinations of the parents should be as recent as possible and certainly no older than six months before the birth date of the Cavalier you are considering purchasing. See *www.premiercavalierinfosite.com/ mitralvalvedisease.htm* for examples of how health clearance forms look.

Syringomelia: Up to 95 percent of Cavs have some degree of the skull malformation that causes syringomelia, and up to 50 percent actually develop the condition, which is potentially painful and even paralyzing. The leading Cavalier syringomelia experts recommend that all Cavaliers should be MRI screened before being bred; any dog screened before age $2^1/2$ years should have a second screening when older. According to the age at testing and the test results, dogs are categorized as follows:

Hip dysplasia: As many as one third of Cavaliers may have hip dysplasia, a potentially laming disorder of the hip joint. You cannot tell whether a dog is dysplastic or not by watching how he walks—only by X-raying the hips. All breeding stock should have hips X-rayed after two years of age with the results evaluated by the Orthopedic Foundation for Animals (OFA) or PennHip. You can look up results at *www.offa.org*. Some copies of official hip dysplasia registry forms can be seen at: *www. premiercavalierinfosite.com/hipdysplasia.htm*.

Patellar luxation: This condition is common in small breeds, but not so much in Cavaliers. About 2.5 percent of Cavs recorded with the Orthopedic Foundation for Animals have patellar luxation. It is relatively simple to screen for, and all breeding stock should have written certification that they are clear of the problem.

Eyes: About 30 percent of Cavaliers have eye problems, some of which can be blinding. Breeding stock should have their eyes checked within one year before breeding, and certified as free from hereditary eye disease by an ophthalmologist using forms provided by the Canine Eye Registration Foundation (CERF: *www.vmdb.org/history.html*).

Hearing: Some Cavaliers have hereditary deafness. Breeding stock should have a Brainstem Auditory Evoked Response (BAER) test some time after age two and be certified free of deafness.

Blood tests: Some Cavaliers have diabetes mellitus or hypothyroidism, both conditions that are easily checked with blood tests. Because they can appear at a later age, breeding stock should be checked within a year before breeding. The breeder should have documentation from the veterinarian showing normal results.

Neurological conditions: Ask the breeder if either parent has suffered from seizures or episodic falling (see pages 70–71). Neither of these conditions has a test available, so you must rely on the honesty of the breeder in this case.

Without an MRI, testing will typically run a couple of hundred dollars in the United States, several hundred more with an MRI. That's why puppies from health-tested stock are expensive, or should be expensive, compared to those from stock that hasn't been tested. Having parents that test clear doesn't do away with the possibility that your puppy might inherit one of these conditions, but it does greatly reduce the chance. And that extra assurance is invaluable.

There will be breeders who will tell you that health testing is just a marketing ploy, that it's overrated, that it's unnecessary, or that they don't need to do it because their dogs have never had any genetic defects or health problems, but those statements should all raise red flags. Nor should a breeder be insulted when you ask for documentation of heath tests results—after all, any smart breeder would be shoving those results at you after what they've paid for them!

Note: These tests or the board-certified specialists who perform them may not be readily available to Cavalier breeders in all parts of the world, so allowances must be made.

Further resources can be found at *www.cavalierhealth.org* and *www.premiercavalierinfosite.com*.

Price

Cavaliers are expensive. At this time, a well-bred Cavalier puppy from health-tested parents in the United States will cost between $1,500 and $3,000, with $1,800 to $2,500 most typical. A Cavalier from a backyard breeder, without health-tested parents, may run from $500 to $800.

Don't fall for the recent ruse of foreign-bred imports being offered at cheap prices. These puppies are raised under poor conditions,

CHECKLIST

Buyer Beware

✔ Avoid breeders who insist on meeting you anywhere except their own home or kennel.

✔ Avoid breeders who will not let you meet the dam of the puppies.

✔ Avoid brokers who act as intermediaries between breeders and buyers. Especially avoid brokers who are importing dogs from foreign countries.

✔ Avoid breeders who do not heart test, or will not provide documentation.

✔ Avoid breeders who always have Cavaliers available of all ages and colors.

✔ Avoid breeders who have many different breeds of dogs.

✔ Avoid breeders whose dogs are not registered with the AKC, CKCSC-USA, or the UKC, or if foreign, with the national kennel club in their country. Do not be fooled by the many other registries that will register any dog for a fee.

separated from their dams at too early an age, and brought en masse to America by puppy brokers.

Good Breeders

Responsible breeders don't sell puppies except to people they have met and interviewed. That means that puppies advertised through stores or third parties probably aren't from good breeders. Because Cavaliers command high prices, some unethical breeders churn out as many litters as they can, cutting as many corners as possible in hopes of turning a profit. Their puppies come from parents with no health testing or health care, and are raised in deplorable conditions with no socialization. If you can't see photos of at least the sire and dam, you're probably not getting a puppy that was bred with quality and health as a priority. Even though you simply want a companion, it's in your best interest to buy from a responsible breeder who breeds for quality Cavaliers. Such breeders usually have companion-quality dogs that look just as beautiful, have just as good personalities, are just as healthy, and have been raised with the same love and care as their next Best in Show prospect.

Look for responsible breeders exhibiting at dog shows, especially Cavalier specialty shows. The two parent clubs can give you a list of breeders in your area (see *www.ackcsc.org/breeder.htm* and *www.ckcsc.org.*) Another place to start is the Cavalier Info Center breeder's list at *www.premiercavalierinfosite.com/buyingapuppy.htm.*

Once you've made up your mind, it's natural to be in a hurry to get your new Cavalier. But good breeders have waiting lists for puppies. Even if they happen to have one available, good breeders don't let Cavalier puppies leave for new homes until they are 8 to 12 weeks old.

Rescue

Responsible breeders provide a home for the dogs they breed for life should their new owners not be able to keep them. But not all Cavaliers are bred by responsible breeders, and even responsible breeders sometimes have unforeseen circumstances and can't take back a dog.

Cavaliers end up in rescue for many reasons. Some owners find their dogs demand too much

CHECKLIST

Breeder Checklist

Responsible breeders:

✔ breed only one or two breeds of dogs, so they can concentrate on just those breeds.

✔ breed no more than three or four litters per year, so they can concentrate on those litters.

✔ can compare their dogs objectively to the Cavalier standard.

✔ can discuss Cavalier health concerns and provide evidence of the health of their own dogs.

✔ can give substantial reasons relating to quality of conformation, temperament, and health why they bred the litter or chose those parents.

✔ have pictures of several generations of the puppy's ancestors.

✔ have clean, friendly, healthy adults.

✔ have clean facilities that promote inter-action with their dogs.

✔ raise their litter inside the house and underfoot, not in a kennel or garage.

✔ question you about your facilities, your prior experiences with dogs, and your intentions regarding your new dog.

✔ sell companion-quality puppies only with limited registration, which means their progeny cannot be registered.

✔ insist upon taking the dog back should you be unable to keep it at any time during its life.

of their time, or consider the Cav's desire to stay close to be overly needy for what they can live with. Some owners find their dogs have medical conditions they're not willing or able to pay for. Some owners die, some have unforeseen circumstances, and some simply tired of having a dog. Some were used as breeding stock in puppy mills and have been discarded because they're past their prime. Whatever the reason, rescue Cavaliers are filled with love but have no one on whom to lavish it. Occasionally they have behavior problems, often stemming from poor training or socialization, but good rescue organizations will make sure you know any problems ahead of time and will help you guide your Cavalier to becoming the best dog he can be. Rescue Cavaliers range from the occasional puppy to the more common middle-aged or senior dog, but have in common a need for a forever home they can call their own (see page 93 for a list of Cavalier Rescue groups).

THE KING AND I

*After finally choosing your Cavalier
pup, it's only natural to want to bring
it home right away. But not so fast!
It will be a lot easier to puppy-proof
your home now than it will be when
your tail-wagging scalawag is
underfoot undoing everything as
fast as you can do it!*

A Cav's Home Is Her Castle

The Cavalier can thrive in either an apartment or a house, so long as you do your part to make both your dog and your home safe.

Outside: Unless you plan to walk your dog on a leash every time you take her outdoors, a secure fence should be your priority safety item. The Cavalier seems unable to comprehend that anything could harm it, and so will stand trustingly in the path of a speeding car.

Your fence must not only be strong enough to keep your dog in, but to keep stray dogs out. This is why the "invisible fences" that keep your dog within are less than optimal, especially for small dogs. These barriers work only with a dog that is wearing a special shock collar that is activated by the buried boundary wire. They can't keep out stray dogs that aren't wearing such a collar.

Dangers can still loom within the yard. If you leave your Cavalier alone in your yard, lock your gate and take precautions against making your defenseless friend a target for thieves.

Check for poisonous plants, bushes with sharp, broken branches at Cavalier eye level, and trees with dead branches or heavy fruits in danger of falling. If you have a pool, be aware that, although dogs are natural swimmers, a little Cavalier cannot pull itself up a swimming pool wall and can drown.

Inside: The first step in dog-proofing your home is to do everything you would to baby-proof your home. Get down at puppy level and see what dangers beckon.

✔ Puppies love to chew electrical cords and even lick outlets. These can result in death from shock, severe burns, and loss of jaw and tongue tissue. Hide cords behind furniture, and coat those you can't hide with an antichew preparation.

✔ Jumping up on an unstable object (such as a bookcase) could cause it to come crashing down, perhaps crushing the puppy.

✔ Do not allow the puppy near the edges of high decks, balconies, or staircases. Use temporary plastic fencing or chicken wire in dangerous areas.

Cavalier-proof your home inside and out before your new puppy has a chance to find trouble on her own.

puppy left alone can be an accomplished one-dog demolition team. Leather furniture is the world's biggest rawhide chewy, and wicker can provide hours of chewing enjoyment (and danger from splintering). Puppies particularly like to chew items that carry your scent. Shoes, eyeglasses, and clothing must be kept out of the youngster's reach. Remove books and papers. No need for a costly paper shredder when you have a puppy!

The Homecoming Kit

It's not really true that "all you need is love" (but you'll need lots of that, too)! Best sources for accessories are large pet stores, dog shows, and discount pet catalogs. Here is your welcome basket checklist.

✔ Buckle collar: for wearing around the house.
✔ Martingale collar or harness: safer for walking on lead.
✔ Leash: nylon, web, or leather—never chain! An adjustable show lead is good for puppies.
✔ Lightweight retractable leash: better for older adult; be sure not to drop the leash as it can retract toward the puppy and frighten it.
✔ Stainless steel flat-bottomed food and water bowls: avoid plastic; it can cause allergic reactions and hold germs.
✔ Crate: just large enough for an adult to stand up in without having to lower its head.
✔ Exercise pen: tall enough that an adult can't jump over.
✔ Toys: fleece-type toys, balls, stuffed animals, stuffed socks. Make sure no parts of toys,

✔ Doors can be a danger area. Everyone in your family must be made to understand the danger of slamming a door, which could catch a small dog and break a leg—or worse. Use doorstops to ensure that the wind does not blow doors suddenly shut, or that the puppy does not go behind a door to play. This can be a danger, because the gap on the hinged side of the door can catch and break a little leg if the door is closed. Be especially cautious with swinging doors; a puppy may try to push one open, become caught, try to back out, and strangle. Clear glass doors may be hard to see, and the puppy could be injured running into them. Never close a garage door with a Cavalier running around. Finally, doors leading to unfenced outdoor areas should be kept securely shut.

As much as your Cavalier may try to be good, it's your duty to remove her from temptation. A including squeakers or plastic eyes, can be pulled off and swallowed.

✔ Chewbones: the equivalent of a teething ring for babies; nylon chewbones are preferable to rawhide.

✔ Antichew preparations, such as Bitter Apple. The unpleasant taste dissuades puppies from chewing on sprayed items.

✔ Baby or specially made dog gate(s): better than a shut door for placing parts of your home off limits. Do not use the accordion style, which could choke a dog.

✔ Brush and comb.

✔ Nail clippers.

✔ Poop scoop: Two-piece rake type is best for grass.

✔ Dog shampoo (see page 54 for choices).

✔ First aid kit (see page 66 for contents).

✔ Food: start with the same food the pup is currently eating.

✔ Dog bed: a round fleece-lined cat bed is heavenly, but you can also use the bottom of a plastic crate, or any cozy box with padding. Wicker will most likely be chewed to shreds.

The Den

Just as you find peace and security as you sink into your own bed at night, your puppy needs a place that it can call its own, a place it can seek out whenever the need for rest and solitude arises. That place is her crate. Used properly, your Cavalier will come to think of her crate not as a place to be kept in, but as a place where others are kept out!

A crate is the canine equivalent of an infant's crib. It is a place for naptime, a place where you can leave your puppy without worry of her hurting herself or your home. It is not a place for punishment, nor is it a storage box for your dog when you're through playing with her. Place the crate in a corner of a quiet room, but not too far from the rest of the family. Place the puppy in the crate when she begins to fall asleep and she will become accustomed to using it as her bed. Be sure to place a soft blanket in the bottom. And by taking the puppy upon awakening directly from the crate to the outdoors, the crate will be one of the handiest house-training aids at your disposal.

Note: Don't let your puppy have the run of the entire house. Choose an easily puppy-proofed room where you spend a lot of time, preferably one that is close to a door leading outside. Kitchens and dens are usually ideal. When you must leave your dog for some time, you may wish to place her in a crate, X-pen,

secure room, or outdoor covered kennel. Bathrooms have the disadvantage of being so confining and isolated that puppies may become destructive; garages have the disadvantage of also housing many poisonous items.

A Red Carpet Welcome

Schedule your new puppy's homecoming during a period when you will have several days to spend at home. But don't make the mistake of spending every moment with the new dog. Accustom the youngster to short times away from you, so that when you do leave the house the puppy won't be too upset.

When you get home, put the puppy on lead and carry her to the spot you have decided will be her toilet area. Note that the toilet area is not the play area. Once the puppy relieves herself, praise and give her a tidbit, then take her to another area of the yard to let her explore a little. Your puppy will probably be hungry, so offer her a small meal once inside. Once the puppy has eaten, she will probably have to relieve herself again, so take her back out to the toilet area and remember to praise and give a tidbit for a job well done. When your puppy begins to act sleepy, place her in her crate so that she knows this is her special bed. A stuffed toy, ticking clock, or even plastic milk carton filled with warm water may help alleviate some of the anxiety of being left alone. You may wish to place the crate in your bedroom for this first night so that the puppy may be comforted by your presence. Remember, this is the scariest thing that has ever happened in your puppy's short life; she has been uprooted from the security of a mother, littermates, and loving breeder, so you must be comforting and reas-

Cradle the pup under its chest and rear, and hold it securely next to your own body.

suring on this crucial first night.

The first day with you is not the time for all the neighbors to come visiting. You want your puppy to know who her new family members will be, and more people will only add to the youngster's confusion. Nor is it the time for rough-and-tumble play, which could scare the puppy. Introductions to other family pets might also be better postponed. Why make a confusing and stressful experience even more overwhelming?

Creating a Civilized House Dog

Your puppy now faces the transition from canine litter member to human family member. Every day will be full of novel experiences and new rules. Your puppy is naturally inquisitive and will need you to guide her toward becoming a well-mannered member of the household.

Off-limits training: Before bringing your puppy home you should decide what parts of your home will be off limits. Make sure that every family member understands the rules, and that they understand that sneaking the puppy onto off-limit furniture, for example, is not doing the puppy any favor at all. Your puppy will naturally want to explore every nook and cranny of your house. Part of the puppy's exploratory tools are her teeth, and any chewed items left in her wake are your fault, not your puppy's—you are the one who should have known better. Harsh corrections are no more effective than a tap on the nose along with a firm *"No"* and removal of the item. If you come across one of your cherished items chewed to bits and feel compelled to lash out, go ahead— hit yourself in the head a few times for slipping up. It may teach you a lesson!

Cavaliers naturally consider your chairs and sofas to be their thrones, but if you don't want them on the furniture keep them off from the beginning. Don't pick the puppy up to sit on your lap; instead, sit on the floor with her. Don't fling the puppy off furniture or use mousetraps on furniture surfaces, because both practices are dangerous and absolutely a bad idea unless you like emergency visits to the veterinarian. There are several more humane items (available through pet catalogs) that emit a loud tone when a dog jumps on furniture, but these should not be necessary if you train your young puppy gently and consistently from the beginning.

House-training

Because dogs are creatures of habit, house-training is more a matter of prevention than correction. To avoid accidents, learn to predict when your puppy will have to relieve herself. Immediately after awakening and soon after heavy drinking or playing, your puppy will urinate. You will probably have to carry a younger baby outside to get her to the toilet area on time. Right after eating, or if nervous, your puppy will have to defecate. Circling, whining, sniffing, and generally acting worried usually signals that defecation is imminent. Even if the puppy starts to relieve herself, quickly but calmly scoop her up and carry her outside (the surprise of being picked up will usually cause the puppy to stop in midstream, so to speak). You can also clap your hands or make a loud noise to startle the pup so that she stops. You can add a firm *"No,"* but yelling and swatting are actually detrimental. When the puppy does relieve herself in her outside toilet, remember to heap on the praise and let your Cavalier

It takes work to create a perfectly house-trained dog.

know how pleased you are. Adding a food treat really gets the point across. Keep some in a jar near the door and always accompany your puppy outside so that you can reward her.

Puppies tend to defecate and urinate in areas where they can smell that they have relieved themselves before. This is why it is critical never to let the puppy have an accident indoors; if she does, clean and deodorize the spot thoroughly and block her access to that area. Use a pet deodorizer cleaner, and never use one containing ammonia. Ammonia is a component of urine, so using an ammonia cleaner is like posting a sign that says "go here"!

The number one house-training mistake made by most puppy owners is to give their puppies too much unsupervised freedom in the house. All canines have a natural desire to avoid soiling their den area. As soon as young wolves are able to walk, they will teeter out of their den to relieve themselves away from their bedding. Since you are using a crate for your puppy's den, your Cavalier will naturally try to avoid soiling it. The den area is considerably smaller than your house, however, and it will take some training before your puppy extends the notion of den to your entire home.

Puppies have very weak control over their bowels, so if you don't take them to their elimination area often, they may not be able to avoid soiling. Puppies, like babies, have to eliminate a lot. You can't just stick them in a crate all day while you are at work and think you won't return home to a messy crate and messy puppy. A rule of thumb is that a puppy can, at most, hold its bowels for as many hours as it is months old. This means that a three-month old can hold itself for three hours. If the puppy is forced to stay in a crate longer, so that she can't hold herself and has to soil the crate, you are setting the stage for a big problem. Once she gets used to eliminating in her crate, it may continue. Further, if the crate is too large, the puppy may simply step away from the area she sleeps in and relieve her self at the other end of the crate. An overly large crate can be divided with a secure barrier until the puppy is larger or house-trained.

The number two house-training mistake made by dog owners is overuse of punishment. Even if you catch your dog in the act, overly enthusiastic correction tends only to teach the dog not to relieve herself in your presence, even when outside. This is why you should reward with a tidbit when she does relieve herself outside. Punishment doesn't make clear what is desired behavior, but reward makes it clear very quickly. Punishing a dog for a mess she has made earlier is totally fruitless; it only succeeds in convincing the dog that every once in a while, for no apparent reason, you are apt to go insane and attack her. It is a perfect recipe for ruining a trusting relationship. That "guilty" look you may think your dog is exhibiting is really fear that you have once again lost your mind.

The number three house-training mistake owners make is to open the door and push the puppy outside by herself. After five minutes, the puppy is let back in and promptly relieves herself on the rug. Bad dog? No, bad owner. Chances are the puppy spent her time outside trying to get back inside to her owner. Puppies do not like to be alone, and knowing you are on the other side of the door makes the outside unappealing. If the weather was bad, she prob-

ably huddled against the door so she wouldn't miss when it was again opened. The solution? You must go outside with her every time. Don't take her for a walk, don't play with her, simply go with her to her relief area, say "hurry up" (the most popular choice of command words), and be ready to praise and perhaps give a treat when she does her deed. Then you can play or go back inside.

If you cannot be with your puppy for an extended period, you may wish to leave her outside (weather permitting) so that she will not be forced to have an indoor accident. If this is not possible, you may have to paper-train your puppy. Place newspapers on the far side of the room (or X-pen), away from the puppy's bed or water bowl; near a door to the outside is best. Place the puppy on the papers as soon as she starts to relieve herself.

A better option is to use sod squares instead of newspapers. Place the sod on a plastic sheet, and when soiled, take it outside and hose it off. By using sod, you are training the puppy to relieve herself on the same surface she should eventually use outside. Place the soiled squares outside in the area that you want your dog to use.

As soon as you are hopeful your precocious puppy is house-trained, she will take a giant step backward and convince you there is no link between her brain and bowels. Most people have unrealistic expectations of their dog's ability to become house-trained, based in part upon friends' boasting about their little genius that was house-trained at two days of age or something similarly ludicrous. No matter how wonderful and smart your Cavalier is, she probably will not have full control over her elimination until she is around six months of age, and probably won't be reliably house-trained until a year old—or more! Keep up your training and things really will get better.

If things don't get better, or if your previously house-trained adult Cavalier soils the house, consider the following possible causes:

✔ Some dogs defecate or urinate as an expression of separation anxiety; you must treat the anxiety to cure the symptom. Dogs that mess their crate when left in it are usually suffering from separation anxiety or anxiety about being closed in a crate. Other telltale signs of anxiety-produced elimination are drooling, scratching, and escape-oriented behavior. You need to treat separation distress (see page 34) and start crate training over, placing the puppy in it for a short period of time and working up gradually to longer times. Some dogs that suffer from crate anxiety but not separation distress do better if left loose in a dog-proof room.

✔ Submissive dogs, especially young females, may urinate upon greeting you; punishment only makes this "submissive urination" worse. For these dogs, keep greetings calm, don't bend over or otherwise dominate the dog, and usually this can be outgrown as the dog gains more confidence.

✔ Sometimes a house-trained dog will be forced to soil the house because of a bout of diarrhea, and afterward will continue to soil in the same area. If this happens, restrict the dog from that area and revert to basic house-training lessons once again. Deodorize the area with an enzymatic cleaner (free of ammonia).

✔ Dogs sometimes lose control because of a bladder infection; several small urine spots (especially if bloody or dark) are a sign that a trip to the veterinarian is needed. In fact, a physical examination is warranted any time a formerly house-trained dog begins to soil the house.

✔ Older dogs simply do not have the bladder control that they had as youngsters; paper-training or a doggy door is the best solution for them.

✔ Older spayed females may "dribble"; ask your veterinarian about drug therapy.

✔ Male dogs may "lift their leg" inside the house as a means of marking it as theirs. Castration will often solve this problem as long as it is performed before the habit has become established; otherwise diligent deodorizing and the use of some dog-deterring odorants (available at pet stores) may help. A tube-shaped doggy diaper, available at dog shows, can help incorrigible males.

Royal Pains

One glance into those big innocent eyes and it is hard to believe that your Cavalier could ever do anything wrong. But even the best of dogs with the best of owners can sometimes do the worst of things. Before despairing, consult a certified canine behaviorist (not a local dog trainer), who may employ a combination of conditioning and drug therapy to achieve a cure.

Misuse of punishment is a major cause of continuing problems. If punishment doesn't work the first time, why do owners think that it will work the second, third, or fourth time?

Jumping up: Puppies naturally greet their mother and other adult dogs by licking them around the corners of their mouth. This behavior translates to humans, but to reach your face they need to jump up on you. Sometimes owners love this display of affection, but not when they are all dressed up or when company comes. But you can't expect your Cavalier to know the difference. Instead, teach your dog to sit and stay, and then be sure to kneel down to

TIP

Speaking the King's English

Dubbed "man's best friend," our dogs are expected to understand us without our bothering to learn their language. With very little effort, you can meet your Cavalier halfway. Like their wolf ancestors, Cavaliers depend upon facial expressions and body language in social interactions.

✔ A yawn is often a sign of nervousness. Drooling and panting can indicate extreme nervousness (as well as carsickness).

✔ A wagging tail, lowered head, and exposed teeth upon greeting is a sign of submission.

✔ The combination of a lowered body, wagging tucked tail, urination, and perhaps even rolling over is a sign of extreme submission.

✔ The combination of exposed teeth, a high, rigidly held tail, raised hackles, very upright posture, stiff-legged gait, direct stare, forward-raised ears, and perhaps lifting a leg to urinate indicates very dominant, possibly threatening behavior.

✔ The combination of a wagging tail, front legs and elbows on the ground and rear in the air, is the classic "play-bow" position, and is an invitation for a game.

its level for greetings. When your Cav does jump up, simply say "No" and step backward, so that her paws meet only air. Teaching your dog a special command that lets her know it's OK to jump up (when you're in your grubby clothes) can actually help her differentiate.

Shutting your dog in another room when guests arrive will only make her more crazed to greet people, and ultimately worsen the problem. The more people she gets a chance to greet politely, the less excited she will be about meeting new people, and the less inclined she will be to jump up. Have your guests kneel and greet your sitting Cavalier.

Barking: Having a doggy doorbell can be handy, but there is a difference between a dog that will warn you of a suspicious stranger and one that will warn you of the presence of oxygen in the air. The surest way to make your neighbors dislike your dog is to let her create a racket. Allow your Cav to bark momentarily at strangers, and then call her to you and praise her for quiet behavior, distracting it with an obedience exercise if need be.

Isolated dogs will often bark as a means of getting attention and alleviating loneliness. Even if the attention gained includes punishment, the dog will continue to bark in order to obtain the temporary presence of the owner. The simplest solution is to move the dog's quarters to a less isolated location. For example, if barking occurs when your Cav is put to bed, move her bed into your bedroom. If this is not possible, the puppy's quiet behavior must be rewarded by the owner's presence, working up to gradually longer and longer periods. The distraction of a special chew toy, given only at bedtime, may help alleviate barking. The puppy that must spend the day home alone is a greater challenge. Again, the simplest solution is to change the situation, perhaps by adding another animal—a good excuse to get two Cavaliers! But warning: Some Cavaliers also like to bark when playing!

Separation distress: This is one of the most common, and commonly misunderstood, Cavalier behavior problems. The Cavalier is an extremely devoted dog, and its owners are typically extremely devoted people. They chose a Cavalier in part because of the breed's desire to be close to its people. The problem is, for many dogs, the people go off and desert them on a regular basis. Dogs are highly social animals, and being left alone is an extremely stressful condition for many of them. They react by becoming agitated and trying to escape from confinement. Perhaps they reason that if they can just get out of the house they will be reunited with their people. The telltale signature of a dog suffering from separation anxiety is that most of its destructive behavior is focused around doors and windows. Most owners believe the dog is "spiting" them for leaving it, and punish the dog. But dogs *never* destroy out of spite. Punishment is ineffective because it actually increases the anxiety of the dog, as it comes to both look forward to and dread its owner's return.

The proper therapy is treatment of the dog's fear of being left alone. This is done by leaving the dog alone for very short periods of time and gradually working to longer periods, taking care never to allow the dog to become anxious during any session. When you *must* leave the dog for long periods during the conditioning program, leave it in a different part of the house than the one in which the conditioning sessions take place, so that you don't undo all your work by letting the dog become over-stressed by your long absence.

In either case, when you return home, no matter what the condition of the home, greet the dog calmly or even ignore her for a few minutes, to emphasize the point that being left was really no big deal. Then have the dog perform a simple trick or obedience exercise so that you have an excuse to praise her. It takes a lot of patience, and often a whole lot of self-control, but it's not fair to you or your dog to let this situation continue. Separation anxiety is really a type of fear: the fear of being left alone.

Puppies are natural demolition dogs, and the best cure is adulthood. Adult dogs still may dig or destroy items through frustration or boredom. The best way to deal with these dogs is to provide both physical interaction (such as chasing a ball) and mental interaction (such as practicing a few simple obedience commands) on a daily basis.

Fearfulness: Despite their generally fearless attitude, Cavaliers can develop phobias and other fears. Fearfulness can be prevented to a great extent by early socialization of your puppy. Once she is vaccinated, take her on outings where she will meet friendly people and well-behaved dogs. Go to the park, puppy kindergarten classes, or for walks in the neighborhood. Make each encounter a positive one, and never push your dog into situations that might overwhelm her.

✔ Fear of thunder is a common problem in older dogs. Try to avoid it by acting cheerful when a thunderstorm strikes, and play with your dog or give it a tidbit. Once a dog develops a thunder phobia, try to find a recording of a thunderstorm. Play it at a very low level and reward your dog for calm behavior. Gradually increase the intensity and duration of the recording.

✔ Another common fear is a fear of strangers. Never force a dog that is afraid of people to be petted by somebody it doesn't know; it in no way helps the dog overcome its fear and is a good way for the stranger to get bitten. Strangers should be asked to ignore shy dogs, even when approached by the dog. Dogs seem to fear the attention of a stranger more than they fear the strangers themselves. When the dog gets braver, have the stranger offer it a tidbit, at first while not even looking at the dog. A program of gradual desensitization, with the dog exposed to the frightening person or thing and then rewarded for calm behavior, is time-consuming but the best way to alleviate any fear.

✔ Never coddle your dog when she acts afraid, because it reinforces the behavior. It is always useful if your Cavalier knows a few simple commands; performing these exercises correctly gives you a reason to praise the dog and also increases the dog's sense of security because she knows what is expected of her. Whether it is a fear of strangers, dogs, car rides, thunder, or being left alone, the concept is the same: never hurry, and never push the dog to the point that she becomes afraid. Drug therapy may help.

THE COURTEOUS CAVALIER

As an integral member of your family, your Cavalier will need guidance to be a proper little lady or gentleman. Young Cavaliers are natural followers, not leaders. They will elect you as their leader and will expect you to guide them. Don't let them down.

Head of the Class

Dog obedience classes are a good idea for several reasons:

✔ They keep you motivated to stay on schedule.

✔ They are a source of training advice that can tell you what you are doing wrong as no book could ever do.

✔ They provide an environment filled with distractions that are good for polishing your exercises.

✔ They provide a safe venue for your Cavalier's socialization with dogs and people.

✔ And where else could you have so much fun showing off your little genius?

The Right Way to Train

Cavaliers are very amenable to training, but they respond best to gentle techniques. Use the methods the professionals use, and you will be astounded by what your Cavalier can learn.

✔ **Guide, don't force:** Cavaliers already want to please you; your job is to simply show them the way. Forcing them can distract them or intimidate them, actually slowing down learning.

✔ **Correct, don't punish:** Such methods as striking, shaking, choking, and hanging have been touted by some (stupid) trainers: Do not try them! These methods are extremely dangerous, counterproductive, and cruel; they have no place in the training of a beloved family member. Plus, they don't work.

✔ **Correct and be done with it:** Owners sometimes try to make this "a correction the dog will remember" by ignoring or chastising the dog for the rest of the day. The dog may indeed remember that his owner was upset, but he will not remember why. The dog can only relate his present behavior to your actions.

✔ **You get what you ask for:** Dogs repeat actions that bring them rewards, whether you intend this connection or not. Letting your

you just aren't sure what you want from your dog. But lapses in consistency are ultimately unfair to the dog. If you feed your begging dog from the table "just this one time," you have taught him that while begging may not always result in a handout, you never know, it just might pay off tonight. In other words, *you* have taught your dog to beg.

✔ **Say what you mean:** Your Cavalier takes his commands literally. If you have taught that *"Down"* means to lie down, then what must the dog think when you yell *"Down"* to tell him to get off the sofa where he was already lying down? Or *"Sit down"* when you mean *"Sit"*? If *"Stay"* means not to move until given a release word and you say *"Stay here"* as you leave the house for work, do you really want your dog to sit by the door all day until you get home?

✔ **Train before meals:** Your Cavalier will work better if his stomach is not full, and will be more responsive to food rewards. Never try to train a sleepy, tired, or hot dog.

✔ **Happy endings:** Begin and end each training session with something the dog can do well. And keep sessions short and fun—no longer than 10 to 15 minutes. Dogs have short attention spans and you will notice that after about 15 minutes their performance will begin to suffer unless a lot of play is involved. To continue to train a tired or bored dog will result in the training of bad habits, resentment in the dog, and frustration for the trainer. Especially when training a young puppy, or when you have only one or two different exercises to practice, quit while you are ahead! Keep your Cavalier wanting more.

Cav out of his crate to make him quit whining might work momentarily, but in the long run you will end up with a dog that whines incessantly every time you put him in a crate. Make sure you reward only those behaviors you want to see more often.

✔ **Mean what you say:** Sometimes a puppy can be awfully cute when he misbehaves, or sometimes your hands are full, and sometimes

✔ **Name, command, action!** The first ingredient in any command is your dog's name. You probably spend a good deal of your day talking,

with very few words intended as commands for your dog. So warn your dog that this talk is directed toward him.

Many trainers make the mistake of saying the command word *at the same time* that they are placing the dog into position. *This is incorrect.* The command comes immediately *before* the desired action or position. The crux of training is anticipation: the dog comes to anticipate that after hearing a command, he will be induced to perform some action, and he will eventually perform this action without further assistance from you. On the other hand, when the command and action come at the same time, not only does the dog tend to pay more attention to your action of placing him in position, and less attention to the command word, but the command word loses its predictive value for the dog. Remember: Name, command, action, reward!

✔ **Once is enough:** Repeating a command over and over, or shouting it louder and louder, never helped anyone, dog or human, understand what is expected. Your Cavalier is not hard of hearing.

✔ **Think like a dog:** Dogs live in the present; if you punish them they can only assume it is for their behavior at the time of punishment. So if you discover a mess, drag your dog to it from his nap in the other room, and scold, the dog's impression will be that either he is being scolded for napping, or that his owner is mentally unstable. In many ways dogs are like young children; they act to gratify themselves, and they often do so without thinking ahead to consequences. But unlike young children, dogs cannot understand human language (except for those words you teach them), so you cannot explain to them that their actions of five minutes earlier were bad.

━━━━━ **TIP** ━━━━━

Leash

A leash that comes from several feet overhead has virtually no guiding ability whatsoever. You need a lower pivot point for the leash in relation to the dog, and you can achieve this by what is called a "solid leash." This is simply a hollow lightweight tube, such as PVC pipe, about 3 feet (1 m) long, through which you string your leash. To prevent your dog from sitting or lying down, loop part of your regular leash around his belly and hold onto that part, so you have a convenient "handle."

Remember: timing is everything in a correction. If you discover your dog in the process of having an "accident," and snatch the dog up and deposit it outside, and then yell *"No,"* your dog can only conclude that you have yelled *"No"* to it for eliminating outside. Correct timing would be *"No,"* quickly take the dog outside, and then reward him once he eliminates outside. In this way you have corrected the dog's undesired behavior and helped the dog understand desired behavior.

✔ **The best-laid plans:** Finally, nothing will ever go as perfectly as it seems to in all the training instructions. But although there may be setbacks, you *can* train your dog, as long as you remember to be consistent, firm, gentle, realistic, and, most of all, patient.

Training Equipment

Equipment for training should include a 6-foot (2 m) and a 20-foot (6.6 m) lightweight lead. For puppies it is convenient to use one of the lightweight, adjustable-size show leads. Most Cavaliers can be trained with a buckle collar.

Positively Good!

In the bad old days, you pushed and pulled and jerked your dog until he did what you wanted. The whole thing wasn't much fun for either of you, and it didn't work very well. Cavaliers naturally want to please you, but nobody likes to be bullied.

But, just like you, Cavaliers do like to have fun and to be rewarded for their efforts. When you're rewarded enough, you'll go out of your way to do even more than what's asked. New training methods focus on fun, food, and positive associations. They produce happy, well-trained dogs that are eager to learn more.

Punishment

What about punishment? Punishment isn't a good way to teach a dog to do anything. About the only thing it's good for is to teach a dog to do nothing—and if you want a dog that does nothing you should get a stuffed toy dog!

In the old days your dog had to wear a choke, or slip, collar for training. That's because training traditionally involved correcting the dog with a quick snap and release. It wasn't supposed to choke him, but it was supposed to be startling. With positive methods you can use such a collar, but you're just as well off using a buckle collar. You won't be tugging on it. You will want a 6-foot (2-m) leash (not chain!) and maybe a 20-foot (6.6-m) light line. Now you're ready!

Before you start:

✔ Find a quiet place away from distractions. Only when your dog learns a skill very well should you gradually start practicing it in other places.

✔ Don't try to train your dog if he's tired, hot, or has just eaten. You want him peppy and hungry for your fun and treats.

✔ Don't train your dog if you're impatient or mad. You won't be able to hide your frustration, and your dog will be uneasy. Losing your cool one time can undo days of proper training.

✔ Keep your training sessions short—very short. Dogs learn best in 10- to 15-minute sessions.

✔ Always quit while he's still having fun and doing something he can do well. You can train him several times a day if you want.

Most dogs love praise, but, short-term at least, they love food—just as you like praise, but you'd rather get a pay-check for your work. So prepare a lot of tiny treats for rewards, and don't be stingy with them.

Your goal is to get a treat to your dog as quickly as you can after he does something right. That's not always as easy as it sounds, because half the time you're fumbling for it, or by the time you get it to his mouth he's doing something else—and now he thinks you're rewarding him for *that*. So you

You can use a backscratcher to reach your dog without bending down all the time. You can also string your leash through a hollow tube of PVC, to lower the leverage point.

need to have an immediate cue that tells your dog, "Yes, that's right!" You can use a consistent word to tell your dog this: *"Good!"* or *"Yes!"* or even better, an unusual sound that really stands out from the rest of your babble.

No dog learns to do something perfectly at first. You have to gradually teach him, shaping his behavior closer and closer to what you want. By following his behavior with a reward, your dog tries to repeat what he did to get more.

Review

First, review these basics:
• Always train in gradual steps. Give rewards for getting closer and closer to the final trick.
• Give a reward instantly when your dog does what you want. The faster you reward, the easier it is for your dog to figure out what you like.
• Don't forget to praise and pet your dog as part of the reward!
• Say your dog's name just before you give the command cue word so he knows the next word you say is directed at him.
• Give the command cue just before you get the dog to do the behavior, not during or after it.

• Just say a cue word once. Repeating it over and over won't help your dog learn it.
• You'll need a way to make a click sound and many, many tiny treats, such as tiny bits of hot dog.

Sit

The old way of teaching the *sit* was to pull up on your dog's collar and push down on his rear as you said *"Sit."*

It's much easier to lure him into position. With his rear in a corner so he can't back up, take your treat and hold it just above and behind his nose, so he has to bend his rear legs to look up at it. Reward. Repeat several times, then move the treat farther back so he has to bend his legs more. Keep on until he has to sit.

Only when Dabba is sitting reliably to the treat lure do you introduce a cue word: *"Dabba, sit."* Gradually fade out use of the treat lure, using just your hand at first, then nothing. Be sure to continue giving it as his final reward, though. Congratulations—you've taught your Cavalier to sit without jerking on his collar or pushing on his rear. He probably thinks this is pretty fun. He probably would like to learn some other ways to con you out of some good treats. Fortunately, you have some ideas.

Down

In the old days you would teach your Cavalier to lie down by wrestling his front legs to the ground. There's an easier way.

With Dabba sitting or standing, use your treat to lure his nose down and forward. You may have to prevent him from walking forward by gently restraining him with your other hand. Reward for just putting his nose down and forward a bit, then for reaching to the ground, then for lowering his elbows a bit, then for lying all the way down. Then reward only for doing it when you give the cue: *"Dabba, down!"*

Use a treat to lure your dog's head back and slightly up, so his rear goes down.

Stay

Once your dog knows *sit* or *down*, wait a few seconds after he's in position before rewarding. Tell him *"Stay"* (this command doesn't use his name in front of it, because some dogs tend to jump up when they hear their name) and gradually lengthen the time he must stay before getting the click and reward.

You can step out just in front of him to face him, then pivot back in place before rewarding. Go a little farther away, or stay a little longer time, but remember, it's better for him to succeed than to fail, so don't push his limits. If he does get up, simply put him back in position and have him stay a shorter time.

Heel

In the old days you trained dogs to *heel* by letting them forge ahead and then jerking them back into position. This taught the dog to keep an eye on you because you were a menace on a leash. To watch you they tended to lag behind you. *Heeling* was not a happy affair.

Your aim is to have your dog walk abreast of your left leg. If your dog isn't leash-trained, place him on a leash and just walk with him. Reward when he's by your side. Show him a treat and encourage him to walk a few feet with you for it. You can perfect his position if you want a good-heeling dog by rewarding only when he is by your left leg. Again, shape him gradually to get to that point. Once there, introduce the cue: *"Dabba, heel!"*

Come

Your dog already knows how to come when he sees you setting down his dinner. Your job is to make him want to come that eagerly every time you call him. You do this by making it rewarding to come to you. Keep some treats in your pocket, and don't be stingy with them when he comes. Even if he's been up to mischief, be sure not to reprimand him when he comes. Cavaliers are smart enough to figure out they'd be better off staying away next time.

MEALS FIT FOR A KING

Big puppy dog eyes plead for a bite of your meal. Who could refuse? But those sad eyes are at once the Cavalier's most powerful weapon and own worst enemy.

Dog cannot live by chow alone (according to Cavaliers, at least), but too many snacks given "just this once" will turn your little lapdog into a big fat dog. An occasional snack will not harm most dogs, but the problem with giving snacks to a small dog is that all but the smallest morsels take up what little room she has in her stomach for essential nutritious food.

"You are what you eat" is just as true for dogs as it is for people. Because your Cavalier can't go shopping for her dinner, it "will be what you feed her," so you have total responsibility for feeding your dog a high-quality balanced diet that will enable her to live a long and active life. Choosing a dog food is one of the most confusing yet important decisions a dog owner must make.

Despite what your Cavalier would have you believe, you're the best judge of what, when, and even where she should eat.

Cavalier Cuisine

Although dogs are members of the order Carnivora (meat-eating mammals), they are actually omnivorous, meaning their nutritional needs can be met by a diet derived from both animals and plants. Most dogs do have a decided preference for meat over nonmeat foods, but a balanced meal will combine both meat and plant-based nutrients.

Food Choices

Commercial dog foods should meet the Association of American Feed Control Officials' (AAFCO) guidelines for a particular age group of dogs. Almost all commercially available foods have a statement on the container certifying that the food meets AAFCO guidelines. Critics contend that these guidelines are too lenient, and that many pet foods are made from substandard ingredients. Premium dog foods, available from large pet supply chains,

Home-prepared: Home-prepared diets have become increasingly popular. Such diets have the advantage of being fresh and of using human-quality ingredients. If they are prepared according to recipes devised by certified canine nutritionists, they should have the correct proportion of nutrients. Unlike commercial dog foods, such diets are not customarily tested on generations of dogs, which makes them vulnerable to looking healthy on paper but not being properly digested or utilized. They can also be labor-intensive, although large batches can be made and frozen.

BARF: Some people prefer to feed their dogs a BARF (Bones And Raw Food) diet, with the idea that such a diet better emulates that of a wild dog. They point out that nobody ever sees wolves eating from a bag of kibble, or even cooking their catch of the day. They feed raw meaty bones along with vegetables. Although dogs have better resistance to bacterial food poisoning than do humans, such diets have nonetheless occasionally been associated with food poisoning, often from salmonella, in dogs. Commercially available meats may be awash in contaminated liquids. Perhaps the worst problem with the BARF diets, however, is that most people who claim to use them never bother to find a nutritionally balanced diet, but instead rely on friends who advocate a diet of chicken wings or some equally unbalanced diet.

Scraps: What about table scraps? Although too many table scraps can throw off the nutrient balance, a few may actually be healthy—but choose your scraps carefully. Avoid hunks of fat, which can bring on pancreatitis, and avoid the following human foods that are toxic to dogs:

✔ Onions cause a condition in which the red blood cells are destroyed. Eating an entire onion could be fatal.

usually use better-quality ingredients and exceed AAFCO minimums.

1. Commercial foods come in dry, canned, and moist varieties. Dry foods are generally healthiest, provide needed chewing action, are most economical, but tend to be less appealing. Many people mix them with tastier canned foods.

2. Canned foods are usually higher in fat and are tastier.

3. Semi-moist foods are high in sugar and, although handy for travel, lack the better attributes of the other food types.

4. Dog treats may not always meet AAFCO requirements for a complete diet but are fine as supplements.

✔ Chocolate contains theobromine, which can cause death in dogs.

✔ Macadamia nuts cause some dogs to get very ill; the cause isn't understood.

✔ Raisins and grapes have been associated with kidney failure and extreme sudden toxicity in some dogs.

Nutrition

A balanced diet must have minimal amounts of protein, fat, carbohydrates, vitamins, minerals, and water.

Protein provides the building blocks for bone, muscle, coat, and antibodies. Eggs, followed by meats, have higher-quality and more digestible proteins than do plant-derived proteins.

Fat provides energy and aids in the transport of vitamins. Plus it adds taste. Too little fat in the diet (less than 5 percent dry matter) results in dry coats and scaly skin. Too much fat can cause diarrhea, obesity, and a reduced appetite for more nutritious foods.

Carbohydrates abound in plant and grain ingredients. Dogs were the inventors of the low-carb diet, but people have been bulking up their food with low-cost carbohydrates for years. Dogs can't utilize their nutrients from carbohydrates unless the carbs are cooked; even then, they utilize them to different degrees depending on their source. Carbohydrates from rice are best utilized, followed by potato and corn, and then wheat, oat, and beans. Excessive carbohydrates in the diet can cause diarrhea, flatulence, and poor athletic performance.

Vitamins are essential for normal life functions. Dogs require the following vitamins in their diet: A, D, E, B1, B2, B12, niacin, pyridoxine, pantothenic acid, folic acid, and choline. Most dog foods have these vitamins added in

— TIP —

Changing Diets

If you change from one food to another, do it gradually over several days. One of life's great mysteries is why dogs, which can seemingly scarf down garbage can bounty without ill effects, can get upset stomachs simply by switching from one dog food to another.

A few treats from the table won't hurt, but they shouldn't make up more than 10 percent of the diet, and shouldn't contain bones, chocolate, onions, raisins, grapes, or macadamia nuts.

Calories are necessary for your dog to be energetic, but too many can turn her excess energy into fat. Always keep track of your dog's weight, so she can run and jump into old age.

their optimal percentages, so that supplementing with vitamin tablets is rarely necessary.

Minerals help build tissues and organs, and are part of many body fluids and enzymes.

Deficiencies or excesses can cause anemia, poor growth, strange appetite, fractures, convulsions, vomiting, weakness, heart problems, and many other disorders. Again, most commercial dog foods have minerals added in their ideal percentages. It is not a good idea to supplement your dog's diet with minerals, especially calcium.

Fiber, such as beet pulp or rice bran, should make up a small part of the dog's diet. It's often used in weight-loss diets to give the dog a full feeling, although its effectiveness is controversial. Too much fiber causes large stool volume and can impair the digestion of other nutrients.

Water is essential for life. It dissolves and transports other nutrients, helps regulate body temperature, and helps lubricate joints. Dehydration can cause or complicate many health problems. Keep a bowl of clean, cool water available for your Cavalier at all times.

How much of each nutrient should your dog get? It depends. Growing dogs need more protein, active dogs need more protein and fat, fat dogs need more protein and less fat, and sick dogs need reduction or addition of various ingredients according to their illnesses. When comparing commercial food labels, you have to compare their dry matter. Otherwise, the higher the moisture content, the lower the nutrients levels appear.

Feeding Problems

Several diseases can be helped by feeding specially formulated diets. Such diets can greatly add to a sick dog's quantity and quality of life. Dogs with urinary stones, diabetes mellitus, liver disease, congestive heart failure, and kidney disease can benefit from special commercial or home-prepared diets.

Food Allergies

Cavaliers that are allergic to food ingredients are typically allergic to particular proteins. Beef and corn are common culprits. By feeding a bland diet of proteins the dog has never eaten, such as venison, duck, or rabbit, the allergic symptoms (which range from diarrhea to itchiness) should subside. If they do, ingredients are added back one by one until an ingredient is found that triggers the response. You may have to keep your dog on a diet of novel proteins forever—at least until she develops an allergy to it and you must move to another novel protein. Some hypoallergenic diets consist not of novel proteins, but of protein molecules that are too small to cause allergic reactions.

How Much?

Very young puppies should be fed three or four times a day, on a regular schedule. Feed them as much as they care to eat in about 15 minutes. From the age of three to six months, puppies should be fed three times daily, and after that, twice daily. Adult dogs can be fed once a day, but it is actually preferable to feed smaller meals twice a day.

Some people let the dog decide when to eat by leaving food available at all times. If you choose to let the dog "self-feed," monitor her weight to be sure she is not overindulging. Leave only dry food for "self-feeding." Canned food spoils rapidly and becomes both unsavory and unhealthful.

The Fatted Cav

A Cavalier in proper weight should have ribs that can just be felt when you run your hands along the rib cage. Viewed from above, it should have an hourglass figure. There should be no roll of fat over the withers or rump.

If your Cavalier is overweight, switch to one of the commercially available high-fiber, low-fat, and medium-protein diet dog foods, which supply about 15 percent fewer calories per pound. Read the label carefully; many so-called "lite diets" aren't light at all! Make sure family members aren't sneaking the dog forbidden tidbits.

Many people find that one of the pleasures of dog ownership is sharing a special treat with their pet. Rather than giving up this bonding activity, substitute a low-calorie alternative such as rice cakes or carrots. Keep the dog out of the kitchen or dining area at food preparation or mealtimes. Schedule a walk immediately following your dinner to get your dog's mind off your leftovers; it will be good for both of you.

If your dog remains overweight, seek your veterinarian's opinion. Heart disease and some endocrine disorders, such as hypothyroidism or Cushing's disease, or the early stages of diabetes can cause the appearance of obesity and should be ruled out or treated. A potbelly on a lean body is usually a sign of disease, not overeating. However, most cases of obesity are simply from eating more calories than are expended. Obesity predisposes dogs to joint injuries and heart problems.

A sick or recuperating dog may have to be coaxed into eating. Cat food or meat baby food are both relished by dogs and may entice a dog without an appetite to eat.

Most Cavaliers are "easy-keepers," meaning they eat readily, are not finicky, and also seem to maintain their weight at an optimal level.

THE CAVALIER COIFFURE

You have in your home two powerful weapons with which to keep your Cavalier's coat fragrant and tangle-free. They are a bathtub and a hairbrush.

The Cavalier requires only a short grooming session every few days. Grooming is every bit as important for the Cavalier that strolls around the house as it is for the one that struts around the show ring. After all, neither you nor your guests will feel inclined to caress a dog that reeks of "eau de dirty dog."

The Royal Robes

The most important ingredient in Cavalier grooming is cleanliness. The natural oils of the coat tend to deposit themselves with time, gradually attracting dirt. Dirt and oil are key ingredients in matting. Larger bits of debris, such as leaves and twigs, become focal points around which the coat can wrap, and can often be found at the core of a mat. When a full-coated Cavalier comes in from the yard, take the time to brush any leaves and twigs from his coat before they become embedded.

Friction: Another key ingredient in mat formation is friction. Some friction, such as that between the elbow and chest, is unavoidable, but other friction can be caused by the dog's scratching and chewing himself, perhaps in response to fleas. Check mat-prone areas (the base of the ears as well as between the elbows and chest in heavily coated dogs) for early tangling.

Texture and length: Cavalier coats vary in texture and length. Spayed and neutered dogs tend to have more profuse coats with a fluffier texture. Males tend to have heavier coats. Some dogs have more curl in their coats. The curlier, thicker, and fluffier coats tend to mat more easily. For these coats daily grooming may be needed. Use a slicker brush to remove as much undercoat as possible. Although the Cavalier standard states that no trimming should be done, if you find yourself overwhelmed by a heavy coat in a dog you don't

A grooming table makes the job easier.

Grooming

Don't wait until mats have formed to decide something must be done about that coat. Grooming an adult or older puppy that has not been taught how to behave when being groomed is miserable for both of you. Start with a young puppy, one too young to form any tangles or mats. Wait until after the youngster has played and is ready to relax. Use a soft brush all over his body, taking care not to hurt him and to make brushing a pleasurable experience. You can brush the puppy as he lies on your lap or beside you. A grooming table is not really necessary unless you plan to show your Cavalier.

Tools: As the puppy grows older, his coat will bloom and you will need more heavy-duty grooming tools. A pin brush is usually the instrument of choice, supplemented with a wide-toothed comb and the slicker brush (a brush with many bent teeth.) The choice of brush will depend upon your particular dog's coat type. A more fluffy "cotton" coat will be better tamed by a slicker brush, while a silkier coat will be kept under control with a pin

plan to show, you may wish to consult a groomer about trimming or thinning.

Footpads: The bottoms of the footpads should be trimmed on all dogs. Otherwise the long hair can cause the dog to lose traction and slip on slick floors. Even excessive hair growth on the top of the foot can cause slipping if the dog constantly steps on it. This hair also can act as a magnet for dirt and briars, and when damp, can track considerable mud into the house. Again, although the standard is adamant about no trimming, if you don't plan to show your Cavalier, you may wish to trim the foot hair for both safety and maintenance reasons.

Brush the hair in layers, starting at the bottom and going all the way to the skin.

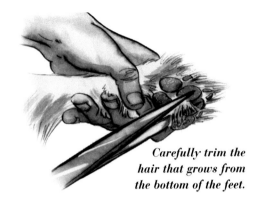

Carefully trim the hair that grows from the bottom of the feet.

Down/Stay

Occasionally have your dog lie in a *down/stay* on his side and groom or examine him. Give him a treat for remaining calm. This is a useful exercise for grooming or veterinary attention. You can even teach a separate command (*"side"*) that means "lie on your side" rather than in the traditional "sphinx" position.

brush. A slicker brush tends to pull more coat out, so if you are trying to nurture every strand, a pin brush is a better choice.

Water: One of the most important brushing tools is actually a spritzer bottle filled with water. Always mist the coat slightly before brushing. This will prevent static electricity from building up, keeping the coat more manageable and less tangle-prone. It will also save the coat by preventing coat breakage while brushing.

Clipping

Although the standard explicitly states the coat should not be trimmed, sometimes your dog will be more comfortable with a haircut. This is especially true for older spayed or neutered dogs, which may grow profuse coats. They'll feel younger and look cute in a trim that is similar to a Cocker Spaniel trim.

Always clip in the direction of hair growth.

✔ Use a #10 blade to clip between the hind legs and forward under the chest. You can leave some longer hair on the sides if you still want the long-haired look without all the thickness.

✔ Use a #7 blade to clip the top of the head, sides of the face, under the chin, and optionally, beneath the ears.

✔ Clip the sides and back of the neck, continuing along the back to the top of the tail, and along the sides about halfway down.

✔ You can use scissors to further shorten and tidy the longer feathering that still remains.

✔ Cutting the longer hair from around the feet will cut down on how much dirt your dog tracks inside.

Shedding Light on Shedding

Shedding is induced not by exposure to warmer temperatures, but by exposure to longer periods of light. This is why indoor dogs, which are exposed to artificial light, tend to shed somewhat all year. Shedding is also under hormonal control. After each estrus or litter, the female will undergo a large-scale shedding process.

Splitting Hairs

When you do come across a tangle or mat, put those scissors away! First get your dog comfortable, and then carefully pull the mat away from the surrounding hair. A light misting of conditioner can help, or working cornstarch into the mat can make it easier to tease apart. Next try to split the mat in half along its long axis, so you now have two smaller mats. Try combing out a little of the mat near its tip, holding the mat near the base with your other hand so you aren't pulling the dog's skin. Then repeat the splitting process, so your original big mat is now four little mats. Continue to alternate combing out the ends and resplitting. In severe cases, you may need to give your dog a time break. Either work on other areas of the dog and then return to the mat at the end of your session, or take a full-fledged play break—as long as you don't forget to finish the job you've started!

Note: If you must use scissors, use them to cut the mat along the same axis along which you would be pulling it apart. Wriggle a comb between the mat and the dog's skin to make sure you don't accidentally cut the dog.

There are two reasons you don't want to just snip the mat out in one chunk. The most obvious is that you are snipping away hair that took a long time to grow, and your dog will look scraggly if you continue to cut away. The less obvious is that as the shorter hairs grow back, they tend to weave themselves back into the longer surrounding hair, so that the area is more likely to then mat over and over.

Bathing Beauties

The two most important rules about bathing are to do it often enough so that the oil and dirt don't create tangles and mats, and never to bathe a dog with any tangles and mats. Bathing a tangle will have the effect of shrinking the hair on itself, creating a mat that will never be brushed free.

You will generally get better results with a shampoo made for dogs. Dog skin has a pH of 7.5, while human skin has a pH of 5.5; bathing in a shampoo formulated for the pH of human skin can lead to scaling and irritation. Most shampoos will kill fleas even if not especially formulated as a flea shampoo, but none has any residual killing action on fleas, so in general, flea shampoos are not a good buy. No Cavalier owner should be without one of the rinse-free shampoos that requires no water or rinsing. These are wonderful for puppies, spot-baths, emergencies, and bathing when time does not permit.

A creme rinse applied to the coat after the bath will cause it to be silkier and more manageable. A silky coat could be rendered too limp and flat by a creme rinse, but a cottony, puffy coat would have better shape and manageability. Creme rinses formulated for dogs are ideal, but you can also use a human creme rinse.

Therapeutic Shampoos

✔ dry scaly skin: moisturizing shampoos
✔ excessive scale and dandruff: antiseborrheic shampoos, often containing tar and sulfur
✔ damaged skin: antimicrobials
✔ itchy skin: oatmeal-based antipruritics
✔ bacterial infections: chlorhexidine shampoos

Sinks

A sink with a hand-held spray makes a handy bathtub. Hold the sprayer against the dog's skin and the dog will not be bothered as much as he would if the spray came from a distance. Use water of a temperature that would be comfortable for you to bathe in, and be sure to keep some running on your own hand to monitor any temperature changes. A fractious puppy could inadvertently hit a faucet knob and cause himself to be scalded. If you keep one hand on your dog's neck or ear, he is less likely to splatter you with a wet dog shake.

Technique

Wet your Cavalier down, working forward from the rear. Once the dog is soaked, use your hand to work in the shampoo; it will go a lot farther and be easier to apply if you first mix the shampoo with warm water. Pay special attention to the oily area around the ear base, but avoid getting water in the dog's ears. Also be careful around the eyes. Rinse thoroughly, this time working from the head back.

Apply creme rinse sparingly. Work it in gently, taking care not to scrub the coat. You need not rinse the creme rinse out of the coat as thoroughly as you rinsed the shampoo.

Drying Out

Squeeze the excess water from your dog's coat, then wrap a towel around him and carry him to a waterproof room where he can shake until the room is soaked.

The best way to dry your Cavalier is with a blow-dryer, brushing the coat from the skin out as the warm air blows upon it. Use warm or even cool air. Hot air can burn the dog's skin, as well as damage the coat. A blow-dryer with a stand is the easiest to use. Blow-dry and brush the dog using the same brushing technique as you do in your normal grooming session.

If your Cavalier's coat is thin, brush the hair backwards as you dry it, so that it tends to stand away from the body. If your Cavalier's coat tends to be thick and wavy, you can blow it dry through a mesh that will hold the coat close to the body. Try placing an old stocking (with the foot cut out and holes cut for the dog's legs) over the dog's body. First brush the wet hair straight. Be sure to dry the ears right to the tips, because otherwise they can mildew, especially in humid weather.

Accustoming your young Cavalier to a blow-dryer can be challenging at first. Start with the dryer away from the head, on a low setting. It helps if it's a cold day and your dog can come to appreciate the warmth of the dryer.

If you can't blow your dog dry you can wrap a towel around him to soak up as much moisture as possible. Keep the dog in a warm room and change the towel often. Finally, if the weather is warm you can let the dog sun dry, but beware: after all that work your nice clean Cav is apt to try to dry himself by rolling in the dirt!

Quick Fixes

✔ Wet or muddy feet can be dried and cleaned by sprinkling a liberal amount of cornstarch into the hair and then brushing it out. You may have to repeat the application a few times.

✔ Pine tar can be loosened with hair spray.

✔ Other tar can be worked out with vegetable oil followed by dishwashing detergent.

✔ Chewing gum can be eased out by first applying ice.

External Parasites

In olden days toy dogs were used to attract fleas from their owners. Today the tables are turned, and it's your job to debug your dog.

Fleas: Fleas are an age-old curse that have only recently been on the losing side. In the past, dog owners sprayed their dogs and yards with poisons until it seemed the people and dogs might die before the fleas did. It was expensive, time consuming, and potentially dangerous. Newer products have a higher initial purchase price but are cheaper in the long run because they work and they need only be reapplied every few months. Look for a product with one of the following ingredients: imidacloprid, fipronil, or selamectin.

Most over-the-counter products are permethrin based, which isn't resistant to water and doesn't kill fleas for long. Flea populations can easily become resistant to it. In fact, fleas can become resistant to any treatment, so the best strategy is to change products frequently and to include the use of both a flea killer and a flea egg killer.

Ticks: Ticks are harder to kill. The same fipronil flea product will kill ticks, but not immediately. Amitraz tick collars are also effective, but not perfect. Regardless, if you're in a tick-infested area you'll need to supplement by feeling your Frenchie daily (she'll like the extra petting), paying close attention around her ears, neck, and between her toes. To remove a tick, use a tissue or tweezers and grasp the tick as close to the skin as possible. Pull slowly, trying not to lose the head or squeeze the contents back into the dog. Even if you get the head with the tick, it will often leave a bump for several days.

Beauty Is Skin Deep

Skin problems in all dogs are the most common problems seen by veterinarians, and the most common of all skin problems is flea allergy dermatitis (FAD). Itchy, crusted bumps with hair loss in the region around the rump, especially at the base of the tail, results from a flea bite anywhere on the dog's body.

Besides FAD, dogs can have allergic reactions to pollens, house dust mites, or other inhaled allergens. Food allergies can also occur.

Pyoderma, with pus-filled bumps and crusting, is another common skin disease. Impetigo is characterized by such bumps and crusting most often in the groin area of puppies. Both are treated with antibiotics and antibacterial shampoos.

In seborrhea, there may be excessive dandruff or greasiness, often with excessive ear wax and rancid odor. Treatment is with antiseborrheic shampoos.

The Hidden Bear Claws

The long hair of the feet may hide the toenails, causing many owners to neglect cutting the nails as often as needed. When you can hear the pitter-patter of clicking nails, that means that with every step the nails are hitting the floor, and when this happens the bones of the foot are spread, causing discomfort and eventually splayed feet and lameness. If dewclaws are left untrimmed they can get caught on things more easily or actually loop around and grow into the dog's leg. You must prevent this by trimming your dog's nails every week or two.

Begin by handling the feet and nails daily, and then cutting the very tips of your puppy's nails every week, taking special care not to cut the "quick" (the central core of blood vessels

Cut the nails as close to the quick as possible, but take care not to cut into it. If you use a nail grinder, place the leg in a nylon stocking first and push the nails through so the long hair doesn't wrap around the grinder head, and just do a little at a time because grinding heats the nail.

and nerve endings). You may find it easiest to cut the nails with your Cavalier lying on his back in your lap. If you look at the bottoms of the nails you will see a solid core culminating in a hollowed nail. Cut the tip up to the core, but not beyond. On occasion you will slip up and cause the nail to bleed. This is best stopped by styptic powder, but if this is not available dip the nail in flour or hold it to a wet teabag.

Taking the Bite Out of Dental Bills

Plaque and tartar are not only unsightly, but contribute to bad breath and health problems. Dry food and hard dog biscuits, rawhide and nylabone chewies are helpful, but not totally effective at removing plaque. Brushing your Cav's teeth once or twice weekly (optimally daily) with a child's toothbrush and doggy toothpaste is the best plaque remover. If not removed, plaque will attract bacteria and minerals, which will harden into tartar. If you cannot brush, your veterinarian can supply cleansing solution that will help to kill plaque-forming bacteria. You may have to have your veterinarian clean your dog's teeth as often as once a year.

Neglected plaque and tartar can cause infections to form along the gum line. The infection can gradually work its way down the sides of the tooth until the entire root is undermined. The tissues and bone around the tooth erode, and the tooth finally falls out. Meanwhile, the bacteria may have entered the bloodstream and been carried throughout the body, causing infection in the kidneys and heart valves. In fact, periodontal disease is a leading cause of heart valve disease in dogs. Neglecting your dog's teeth can do more harm than causing bad breath; it could possibly kill your dog.

Between four and seven months of age, Cavalier puppies will begin to shed their baby teeth and show off new permanent teeth. Often deciduous (baby) teeth, especially the canines (fangs), are not shed, so that the permanent tooth grows in beside the baby tooth. If this condition persists for over a week, consult your veterinarian. Retained baby teeth can cause misalignment of adult teeth. Correct occlusion (bite) is important for good dental health. In a correct Cavalier bite, the top incisors should fit snugly in front of the bottom incisors. Too large a gap between the upper and lower incisors could cause eating difficulties or result in the tongue lolling out of the mouth.

LONG LIVE THE KING!

Don't wait until your dog is sick to choose a veterinarian. Consider availability, emergency arrangements, facilities, costs, ability to communicate, and experience with Cavaliers. Most general veterinarians can provide a wide range of services, but if your dog has a problem that eludes diagnosis or requires specialized treatment, let your veterinarian know if you are willing to be referred to a specialist in that field.

Preventive Medicine

The best preventive medicine is safeguarding your dog against accidents, which means keeping your dog under control when in public, in a secure fence when in the yard, and in a dog-proofed home when inside. Other preventive measures are also needed, however.

Vaccinations

Without well-timed vaccinations your Cavalier can be vulnerable to deadly communicable diseases. Your puppy received her early immunity through her dam's colostrum during the first few days of nursing. As long as your puppy still has that immunity, any vaccinations you give her won't provide sufficient immunity. But after several weeks that immunity begins to decrease. As her immunity falls, both the chance of a vaccination being effective and the chance of getting a communicable disease

rise. The problem is that immunity diminishes at different times in different dogs. So starting at around six weeks of age, a series of vaccinations are given in order to catch the time when they will be effective while leaving as little unprotected time as possible. During this time of uncertainty it's best not to take your puppy where unvaccinated dogs may congregate. Some deadly viruses, such as parvovirus, can remain in the soil for six months after an infected dog has shed virus in its feces there.

This doesn't mean you must load up on every vaccine available. Vaccinations are divided into core vaccines, which are advisable for all dogs, and noncore vaccines, which are advisable for only some dogs. Core vaccines are those for rabies, distemper, parvovirus, and hepatitis (using the CAV-2 vaccine, not the CAV-1, which can cause adverse reactions and is still sold by some feed stores—and no, that CAV

Spaying and Neutering

Unless you aim to be the kind of breeder you were advised to look for (see pages 22–23), your best plan is to enjoy your Cavalier as a companion and leave the breeding to others. Here's why:

✔ An intact (unspayed) female comes into estrus twice a year, usually beginning at around eight months of age. Each heat period lasts for about three weeks, during which she will have a bloody discharge that can ruin your furnishings or necessitate her being crated for three weeks or wearing little britches. Her scent, which she will advertise by urinating as much as possible, will attract canine suitors to your door. If you have an intact male of your own, he will drive you insane with his relentless panting, whining, shaking, and clawing. It will be the longest three weeks of your life.

✔ If you bred a litter, how would you find homes for the puppies? Do you trust that the people who answer your advertisements will give your puppy a home as good as yours? Will you commit to being responsible for that puppy's well-being for the rest of her life? Will you take every puppy back if their new owners should tire of them or otherwise not be able to keep them?

✔ Good Cavalier breeders make these commitments, and more. They screen for hereditary defects, prove their dogs in some form of competition, educate themselves, and stand by their puppies for a lifetime. They often require that buyers neuter or spay their dogs because they know too well the problems dog breeding can create. They also recognize the health advantages that go along with spaying and neutering.

✔ Intact females are at increased risk of developing breast cancer and pyometra, a potentially fatal infection of the uterus. Spaying negates the possibility of pyometra, and spaying before the first season significantly reduces the chance of breast cancer.

✔ Intact males are more likely to develop testicular cancer and prostatitis. The major drawbacks are that each procedure requires surgery and anesthesia, that many spayed and neutered dogs gain weight, and that some spayed females develop urinary incontinence. Talk to your veterinarian and breeder about the pros and cons. In most cases, however, the pros outweigh the cons.

doesn't have anything to do with your Cav!). Noncore vaccines include those for leptospirosis, corona virus, tracheobronchitis, Lyme disease, and giardia. Your veterinarian can advise you if your dog's lifestyle and environment put her at risk for these diseases. Remember, more is not better!

A sample core vaccination protocol for puppies suggests giving a three-injection series at least two weeks apart, with each injection containing distemper (or measles for the first injection), parvovirus, adenovirus 2 (CAV-2), and parainfluenza (CPIV). The series should not end before 12 weeks of age. A booster is given one year later, and then boosters are given every three years. Rabies should be given at 16 weeks of age, with boosters at one- to three-year intervals according to local law.

Boosters: The topic of how frequently boosters should be given is currently under scrutiny. Some owners elect to test their dogs' blood titers to various diseases to see if a booster is needed. A high titer generally indicates protection, but a low titer doesn't mean the dog isn't protected.

Some proponents of natural rearing condemn vaccinations and refuse to use them. They use homeopathic nosodes instead, and point to the fact that their dogs don't get sick as proof that they work. However, their good fortune is probably the result of herd immunity; that is, as long as most other dogs are vaccinated they probably never come in contact with the infectious agents. And no controlled study has ever supported the effectiveness of nosodes. Vaccinations are not without a downside, but they are essential components of your dog's healthy future. Don't take chances.

De-worming

Your puppy should have been checked and de-wormed if necessary before coming home with you. Most puppies have worms at some point because some types of worms lie dormant and protected in the dam until hormonal changes caused by her pregnancy activate them and enable them to infect her puppies. Your Cav can also pick up worms from the ground in places where dogs congregate. The best prevention at home is to clean up feces immediately. Some heartworm preventives also prevent many types of worms. Get your puppy regular fecal checks for worms, but don't de-worm her unnecessarily. Avoid over-the-counter worm medications, which are neither as safe nor effective as those available from your veterinarian.

If you see small, flat, white segments in your dog's stool, she may have tapeworms. Tapeworms are acquired when your puppy eats a flea, so the best prevention is flea prevention. Tapeworms require special medication to get rid of them.

Heartworm Prevention

Heartworms can kill your dog. They are carried by mosquitoes, so if there is any chance of a single mosquito biting your Cavalier she needs to be on heartworm preventive medication. Ask your veterinarian when she should begin taking the medication, as it may vary according to your location. Dogs over six months of age should be checked for heartworms with a simple blood test before beginning heartworm prevention. The once-a-month preventive is safe, convenient, and effective. Treatment is available for heartworms, but it's far cheaper, easier, and safer to prevent them.

Signs of Illness

Being the link between your dog and her doctor is not an easy job. Since your dog can't talk, you have to interpret her behavioral and physical signs.

Behavior Changes

Sick dogs often lie quietly in a curled position. Irritability, restlessness, hiding, clawing, panting, and trembling may indicate pain. Dogs with abdominal pain often stretch and bow. A dog with breathing difficulties will often refuse to lie down or if she does, will keep her head raised. Confusion, head-pressing, or seizures may indicate neurological problems.

Lethargy is the most common sign of illness. Possible causes include
- Infection (check for fever)
- Anemia (check gum color)

- Circulatory problem (check pulse and gum color)
- Pain (check limbs, neck, back, mouth, eyes, ears, and abdomen for signs)
- Nausea
- Poisoning (check gum color and pupil reaction; look for vomiting or abdominal pain)
- Sudden vision loss
- Cancer
- Metabolic diseases

Intake and Output Changes

Changes in eating, drinking, or elimination patterns often indicate illness.

- Ill dogs often experience loss of appetite, although some endocrine disorders may cause increased appetite.
- Increased thirst, usually with increased urination, may indicate kidney disease or diabetes.
- A sudden and frequent urge to urinate, usually in small amounts, perhaps accompanied by signs of pain, may indicate a urinary tract infection. Painful urination, straining to urinate, or blood in the urine may indicate urinary stones. Inability to urinate is a life-threatening emergency.
- Regurgitating food right after eating can indicate an esophageal problem. Vomiting food after it's been in the stomach can indicate poisoning, blockage, or a host of problems. Consult your veterinarian immediately if your dog vomits feces-like matter (which could indicate an intestinal blockage) or blood (which may resemble coffee grounds), has accompanying fever or pain, or if the vomiting lasts more than a few hours.
- Diarrhea can result from nervousness, a change in diet or water, food sensitivities, intestinal parasites, infections, poisoning, or many illnesses. It's not uncommon for dogs to have blood in their diarrhea, but diarrhea with lots

of blood, or accompanied by vomiting, fever, or other symptoms of illness warrants a call to the veterinarian. Bright red blood indicates a source lower in the digestive tract, while dark black tarry stools indicate a source higher in the digestive tract.

Coughing

Coughing can be caused by foreign bodies, tracheal collapse, tumors, kennel cough, and heart disease, among others. Any cough lasting longer than a few days or accompanied by weakness or difficulty breathing warrants a veterinary exam.

- Congestive heart failure causes coughing and breathing difficulties, mainly after exercise and at night and early morning.
- Kennel cough is a communicable airborne disease caused by several infectious agents. It is characterized by a gagging or honking cough, often a week after being around infected dogs.

Physical Changes

Sometimes you need to check over your dog piece by piece.

Mouth: If you think your Cav is sick, one of the first things to check is her gum color. Gums should be a deep pink, and if you press with your thumb, they should return to pink within two seconds after lifting your thumb (a longer time suggests a circulatory problem). Very pale gums may indicate anemia, shock, or poor circulation. Bluish gums or tongue can mean a life-threatening lack of oxygen. Bright red gums may indicate overheating or carbon monoxide poisoning, and yellow gums jaundice. Tiny red splotches may indicate a blood-clotting problem. Tooth and gum problems will often cause bad breath and pain.

The Five-Minute Checkup

Make several copies of this checklist and keep a record of your dog's home exams.

Date _____   Weight _____   Temperature _____   Pulse _____

Is Your Dog
- [ ] Restless?
- [ ] Lethargic?
- [ ] Weak?
- [ ] Dizzy?
- [ ] Irritable?
- [ ] Confused?
- [ ] Bumping into things?
- [ ] Trembling?
- [ ] Pacing?
- [ ] Hiding?
- [ ] Eating more or less than usual?
- [ ] Drinking more than usual?
- [ ] Urinating more or less than usual, or with straining?
- [ ] Having diarrhea?
- [ ] Straining to defecate?_____
- [ ] Just standing with front feet on ground and rear in the air?
- [ ] Vomiting or trying to vomit?
- [ ] Regurgitating undigested food?
- [ ] Gagging?
- [ ] Coughing?
- [ ] Breathing rapidly at rest?
- [ ] Spitting up froth?
- [ ] Pawing at throat?
- [ ] Snorting?
- [ ] Limping? _____

Physical Exam
- [ ] Hydration: Dry sticky gums?
- [ ] Skin that doesn't pop back when stretched?

Gum color:
- [ ] Pink (good)
- [ ] Bright red
- [ ] Bluish
- [ ] Whitish
- [ ] Red spots

Gums:
- [ ] Swellings?
- [ ] Bleeding?
- [ ] Sores?
- [ ] Growths?

Teeth:
- [ ] Loose?
- [ ] Painful?
- [ ] Dirty?
- [ ] Bad breath?

Nose:
- [ ] Thick or colored discharge?
- [ ] Cracking?
- [ ] Pinched?
- [ ] Sores?

Eyes:
- [ ] Tearing?
- [ ] Mucous discharge?
- [ ] Dull surface?
- [ ] Squinting?
- [ ] Swelling?
- [ ] Redness?
- [ ] Unequal pupils?
- [ ] Pawing at eyes?

Ears:
- [ ] Bad smell?
- [ ] Redness?
- [ ] Abundant debris?
- [ ] Scabby ear tips?
- [ ] Head shaking?
- [ ] Head tilt?
- [ ] Ear scratching?
- [ ] Pain?

Feet:
- [ ] Long or split nails?
- [ ] Cut pads?
- [ ] Swollen or misaligned toes? _____

Skin:
- [ ] Parasites?
- [ ] Black grains (flea dirt)?
- [ ] Hair loss?
- [ ] Scabs?
- [ ] Greasy patches?
- [ ] Bad odor?
- [ ] Lumps? _____

Anal and genital regions:
- [ ] Swelling?
- [ ] Discharge?
- [ ] Redness?
- [ ] Bloody urine?
- [ ] Bloody or blackened diarrhea?
- [ ] Worms in stool or around anus? _____
- [ ] Scooting rear?
- [ ] Licking rear? _____

Abdomen:
- [ ] Bloating?

Body:
- [ ] Asymmetrical bones or muscles?
- [ ] Lumps?
- [ ] Weight change?

If you answered "yes" to anything abnormal in the checklist, it's worth a call to your veterinarian. Refer to the text for more information.

Nose: A nasal discharge may indicate a respiratory illness or other disease, or a foreign body or infection of the nose. A cracked nose pad may just be an overly dry nose that needs to be moisturized, or it could be caused by a disease.

Eyes: Squinting or pawing at the eye can arise from pain. Swelling and redness may indicate glaucoma, a scratched cornea, or several other problems. Profuse tear discharge may be caused by a foreign body, scratched cornea, or blocked tear drainage duct. Thick mucus and a dull-appearing surface may indicate "dry eye" (keratoconjunctivitis sicca, or KCS).

Ears: Inflamed or painful ears can result from infection or parasites. See pages 74–75 for more about ears.

Feet: Foot problems can account for limping. Cut long or split nails short (see pages 56–57),

and protect cut pads. Swollen toes could be from infection or an orthopedic problem.

Skin: Parasites, allergies, and infections can cause many skin problems (see page 56). Lumps in the skin may or may not be serious, but warrant a veterinary examination.

Anus: Repeated diarrhea can cause an irritated anal area. Repeated scooting or licking can be from diarrhea; parasites, or especially, impacted anal sacs. The anal sacs are two sacs filled with smelly brown liquid that normally is excreted with the feces or in times of fright. In some cases the material can't get out. This is especially true if the tail twists sharply to one side, which can compress one duct. The sac becomes uncomfortably distended, sometimes becoming infected. It may swell outward, even appearing to be a tumor, and often finally

Medications

✔ To give a pill, open your dog's mouth and place the pill well in the rear of the mouth. Close the mouth and gently stroke the throat until he swallows. Or just hide the pill in some cream cheese or liverwurst and watch to make sure he eats it.

✔ To give liquid medication, place the liquid in the side of the mouth and let the dog lap it down. Don't squirt it in so that the dog inhales it.

✔ Always give the full course of medications prescribed by your veterinarian.

✔ Never give human medications unless your veterinarian tells you to. Some human medications work on dogs but must be used at different strengths, and some have no effect or bad effects on dogs.

burst. Your veterinarian can manually express the contents.

Temperature: To take your dog's temperature, lubricate a rectal thermometer and insert it about 2 inches (5 cm) into the dog's anus, leaving it there for about a minute. Normal is from 101 to 102°F (38–38.9°C). If the temperature is

• 103°F (38.4°C) or above, call your veterinarian for advice. This is not usually an emergency.

• 105°F (40.5°C) or above, go to your veterinarian. This is probably an emergency; 106°F (41°C) or above is dangerous. Try to cool your dog.

• 98°F (36°C) or below, call your veterinarian for advice. Try to warm your dog.

• 96°F (35.6°C) or below, go to your veterinarian. Treat for hypothermia on the way by warming your dog.

Pulse: To check the pulse, cup your hand around the top of your dog's rear leg so your fingers are near the top almost where the leg joins the body. Feel for the pulse in the femoral artery. Normal adult Cav pulse rate is 70 to 120 beats per minute.

Hydration: Check hydration by touching the gums, which should be slick, not sticky, or by lifting the skin on the back and letting it go. It should snap back into place quickly, not remain tented. Sticky gums and tented skin indicate dehydration. If your dog has been vomiting or has diarrhea, she may instantly lose any water you give her, in which case your veterinarian may need to give your dog fluids under the skin, or better, in a vein.

Be Prepared

Because there are no paramedics for dogs, you must assume the role of paramedic and ambulance driver in case of an emergency. Now is the time to prepare for these lifesaving roles.

1. Study the emergency procedures described in this chapter, and keep this guide handy. Misplaced instructions can result in the loss of critical time.

2. Know the phone number and location of the emergency veterinarian in your area. Keep the number next to the phone; don't rely on your memory during an emergency situation.

3. Always keep enough fuel in your car to make it to the emergency clinic without stopping for gas.

4. Finally, stay calm. It will help you help your dog, and will help your dog stay calm as well. A calm dog is less likely to go into shock.

When Confronted with an Emergency

• Make sure breathing passages are open. Remove any collar and check the mouth and throat.
• Move the dog as little and as gently as possible.
• Control any bleeding.
• Check breathing, pulse, and consciousness.
• Check for signs of shock (very pale gums, weakness, unresponsiveness, faint pulse, shivering). Keep the dog warm and calm.
• Never use force; do nothing to cause extreme discomfort.
• Never remove an impaled object unless it is blocking the airway.

Poisoning

Signs of poisoning vary according to the type of poison, but often include vomiting, depression, and convulsions. When in doubt call your veterinarian or an animal poison control hotline (see page 93). If the poison was ingested in the past two hours, and if it's not an acid, alkali, petroleum product, solvent, or tranquilizer, you may be advised to induce vomiting by giving hydrogen peroxide or dry mustard mixed 1:1 with water. Ipecac syrup is not recommended for this purpose in dogs. In other cases you may be advised to dilute the poison by giving milk or vegetable oil. Activated charcoal can absorb many toxins. Poisons act in different ways, so it's important to have the label of any suspected poisons available.

✔ Ethylene glycol-based antifreeze is a dog killer. Even tiny amounts cause irreversible kidney damage, and the prognosis is poor once symptoms appear. Get emergency help if you suspect your dog drank antifreeze.

TIP

Medical Kit

You should maintain a medical kit for your Cavalier, with these items:
• rectal thermometer
• scissors
• tweezers
• sterile gauze dressings
• self-adhesive bandage (such as Vet-Wrap)
• instant cold compress
• antidiarrhea medication
• ophthalmic ointment
• soap
• antiseptic skin ointment
• hydrogen peroxide
• clean sponge
• pen light
• syringe
• towel
• stethoscope (optional)
• oxygen (optional)
• first aid instructions
• veterinarian and emergency clinic numbers
• poison control center number

✔ Rodent poisons are either warfarin-based, which cause uncontrolled internal bleeding, or cholecalciferol-based, which cause kidney failure.
✔ Bird and squirrel poisons are usually strychnine-based, which cause neurological malfunction.
✔ Insect poisons, weed killers, and wood preservatives may be arsenic-based, which cause kidney failure.

Specific Health Information

Most Cavaliers are healthy dogs, but several hereditary health problems can occur.

Heart: Mitral valve disease (MVD) is the leading cause of premature death in CKCSs. Over half of CKCSs over age five have mitral valve murmurs, and virtually all have them by age ten. CKCSs should be screened for murmurs annually, beginning at age one year. Dogs with MVD may benefit from various drugs.

Chiari–like malformation and syringomelia: Up to 95 percent of CKCSs have some degree of caudal occipital malformation syndrome, and as many as 50 percent have some degree of syringomelia as a result. Initial symptoms are itching and pain around the neck and shoulders, in severe cases progressing to weakness and paralysis. A definite diagnosis requires MRI. Drug therapies may alleviate symptoms temporarily; surgery may be successful in halting progression.

Ears: Primary secretory otitis media (glue ear) occurs in CKCSs, producing severe pain and other symptoms that may be confused with syringomelia. In severe cases, the bulging tympanic membrane, or even the mucous plug (if the tympanic membrane has burst) may be seen with an otoscope. Other cases may require MRI or CT imaging. Surgery can relieve the pressure.

Deafness: Congenital and early onset progressive deafness are seen in CKCSs.

Eyes: A CERF study estimated that about 30 percent of CKCSs have eye problems. CKCSs are known to have hereditary cataracts, corneal dystrophy, distichiasis, entropion, keratoconjunctivitis sicca, microphthalmia, retinal dysplasia, and progressive retinal atrophy. Their eyes should be checked annually by an ophthalmologist.

Episodic falling syndrome: Unique to CKCSs, this genetic condition, also called paroxysmal exercise-induced dystonia, causes the dog's muscles to become rigid so that it may have hind leg rigidity, incoordination, or may collapse and be unable to get up. Although it may look seizure-like, the dog is conscious. An episode is usually brought on by excitement, exercise, or stress.

Seizure disorders: Epilepsy is seen in CKCSs, most commonly first occurring between six months and five years of age. Fly-catching syndrome is seen at a high rate in CKCSs. It may be a form of partial seizure, compulsive behavior, or sometimes, a symptom of syringomelia.

Airway: CKCSs may have various degrees of brachecephalic syndrome, most often stenotic nares, elongated soft palate, and everted laryngeal saccules.

Patellar luxation: About 20 percent to 30 percent of CKCSs have some degree of patellar luxation.

Hip dysplasia: As many as one third of all CKCSs have some degree of hip dysplasia. Few become lame from it, however.

Platelets: As many as 50 percent of CKCSs have thrombocytopenia, and 30 percent have macrocytopenia; however, these conditions are not usually associated with abnormal bleeding. Automated counters will underestimate platelet counts. Because the large platelets are fragile, blood should be taken with a large-bore needle from the jugular.

Endocrine disorders: Cushing's disease and diabetes mellitus are seen in the breed at somewhat higher than average rates.

✔ Flea, tick, and internal parasite poisons may contain organophosphates, which can cause neurological symptoms.

✔ Iron-based rose fertilizers can cause kidney and liver failure.

Cavalier Hereditary Problems

Hereditary problems can become widespread in a breed through several mechanisms. One such mechanism is the "founder effect," in which most members of the breed descend from one or a few initial foundation stock, and unfortunately, one or more of those founding fathers (or mothers) carried the defective gene. When the breeding pool is small, closely related individuals must be interbred, increasing the likelihood that recessive deleterious genes will be paired in the resulting offspring.

Today's Cavaliers all descend from six dogs. Unfortunately, at least one of them probably carried genes that resulted in diseases such as syringomelia, episodic falling, and mitral valve disease. When their descendants were interbred, some of the unlucky ones received a combination of genes that resulted in these problems. When the breed was still relatively rare, nobody recognized that there was a breed-related problem. But during the 1970s boom in popularity in Great Britain, it began to be apparent that several problems were occurring in Cavaliers at a greater rate than in most other breeds.

Mitral Valve Disease

Mitral valve disease (MVD) affects far too many Cavaliers. The canine heart consists of four chambers and four one-way valves. The two upper chambers are the left and right atria (singular: atrium), which function as receiving areas for blood returning to the heart. The two lower chambers are the left and right ventricles, which pump the blood out of the heart and throughout the body. The mitral valve controls the flow of blood from the left atrium to the left ventricle.

When the left ventricle contracts, the mitral valve is forced shut, and the blood is pushed through the aorta into the circulatory system. In MVD, the folds of tissue that make up the sides of the mitral valve shrivel and curl, so that the valve no longer closes tightly during the contraction of the left ventricle. The gap in the valve allows the blood to flow backward into the atrium when the left ventricle contracts, a condition termed mitral regurgitation (MR). Because blood flows back into the atrium, the flow to the rest of the body is decreased. The left atrium increases in size in order to accommodate the increased blood volume, and the left ventricle increases in size in order to pump more blood in an attempt to compensate for the decreased blood flow to the rest of the body. As the condition worsens, the left side of the heart becomes increasingly enlarged, and symptoms of congestive heart failure may become evident. Fluid may accumulate in the lungs because of the high pressure in the left atrium causing blood and fluid to back up into the capillaries of the lungs. This fluid accumulation, along with bronchial compression from the enlarged heart, leads to coughing.

Symptoms: In some dogs, few outward symptoms are present, despite increasing deterioration of cardiac function. The first sign to be noted is usually exercise intolerance, but this often goes unnoticed in house pets. Coughing is often the first symptom that owners detect.

Labored or increased rates of breathing may also be present. As the disease progresses, dogs may collapse or faint due to insufficient blood flow to the brain. Symptoms may worsen rapidly, or may progress gradually over a period of years.

Diagnostic tests: Preliminary diagnosis of MVD can usually be made by listening to the heart, preferably by a veterinary cardiologist. With a stethoscope, mitral regurgitation can be detected as a murmur. An electrocardiogram (ECG) can monitor the beats of the heart and record how aberrant they are. The pattern of irregularities can point to problems in different areas of the heart. Many veterinarians can perform an ECG in their office by transmitting the signals to a veterinary hospital specializing in cardiology. Radiographs (X rays) can show whether the heart is enlarged. These can also be done by your local veterinarian. More advanced procedures such as echocardiography can further aid in determining severity.

Treatment: Some affected dogs can still live long lives. Obese dogs should be put on a diet.

Low-sodium diets may be helpful, but their treatment value has not been proved. They are of no value in preventing MVD. Although the progression of the disease cannot be slowed through current means, drugs can help alleviate some of the symptoms. Drug therapies may include diuretics (to reduce fluid accumulation), vasodilators (to expand blood vessels), and other newer drugs.

Inheritance

A 1996 Swedish study demonstrated that parents with valvular disease are more likely to produce offspring with valvular disease. However, the disease did not seem to be inherited in a simple dominant-recessive mode. Instead, it seems to be polygenic in nature, meaning that it depends upon the interplay of many gene pairs. When a sufficient number of deleterious gene pairs are present, they exceed a threshold, and the disease manifests itself in the individual.

The future: Anybody unfortunate enough to have their beloved Cavalier die from MVD

━━━━ **TIP** ━━━━

Finding a Specialist

Your veterinarian can usually set up an appointment for your dog with an appropriate specilist in the event that MVD or syringomelia is suspected. You can also search the list of board-approved cardiologists and neurologists at *www.acvim.org/Specialist/Search.aspx.*

knows too well the grief and frustration of losing a pet too early to a disease for which there was no prevention and no cure.

Several organizations fund research into canine disease, most notably the AKC Canine Health Foundation (*www.akcchf.org*) and the Morris Animal Foundation. You can do your part by contacting these organizations or the Cavalier club and donating toward Cavalier MVD research.

Syringomelia

Almost all Cavaliers have some degree of malformation in the rear of the skull where the skull is slightly too small for the rearmost part of the brain, the part called the cerebellum. This forces a bit of the cerebellum to bulge through the opening in the rear of the skull that the spinal cord goes through. In the process, the cerebral spinal fluid (CSF) that circulates around the brain and down the spine is compressed, causing pockets of fluid called syrinxes to form in the spinal cord. These syrinxes can exert pressure on nerves along the spinal cord, which in turn can cause pain and paralysis. About 30 to 70 percent of all Cavaliers are believed to have syringomelia, but most don't show any significant symptoms.

Symptoms: Symptoms are typically first seen between six months and three years of age, but may appear later or even as early as eight weeks of age. Early symptoms are easy to overlook. They include excessive scratching of the head and neck, especially scratching at the air and while on a leash; tenderness of the neck region, often extending to the head and shoulders, or including the hind legs; weakness or stiffness in the limbs; yelping as if in pain. Dogs with all of these symptoms are especially suspect. A definite diagnosis usually requires a workup by a veterinary neurologist, who will probably order a magnetic resonance image (MRI).

Treatment: If the dog has syringomelia, drug treatment may be tried initially. Surgery may halt the progression of the disease and cause significant improvement, but may not reverse the harm the disease has already done in all cases. About a quarter of all dogs require additional surgery. For an extensive discussion of syringomelia in Cavaliers, see *http://sm.cavaliertalk.com.*

Episodic Falling

This condition, sometimes called collapsing Cavalier syndrome, or more technically, paroxysmal hypertonicity disorder, is often misdiagnosed as seizures or cramps, and many veterinarians aren't even aware of it. In this condition, the muscles contract and can't relax.

Symptoms: The symptoms may be localized and minor, so the dog just moves stiffly, or it may involve many sets of muscles and be more complete, so the dog falls over and can't get up, even though she may be able to struggle. Unlike a seizure, the dog is totally conscious throughout the episode, and when it's over, the dog seems fine. Episodes are more likely to occur when the dog is excited or stressed. In severe cases, the condition becomes chronic, occurring almost randomly. Episodes can last from seconds to minutes. Symptoms usually first occur by age five months, but can occur at any age.

Important: If a dog is having an extended episode, it should be considered an emergency, since the contracting muscles can build up enough heat to cause heatstroke and brain damage.

Treatment: Drug therapy is usually effective in halting an extended episode, and is often effective in reducing the frequency of episodes. Episodic falling is frightening and frustrating for owners, but does not appear to be painful, and most dogs can still enjoy a good quality of life. It is seldom life-threatening. Visit *www. cavalierepisodicfalling.com* for more details.

Hip Dysplasia

Hip dysplasia is a potentially crippling problem in which the head of the femur (thigh bone) doesn't fit properly in the hip socket. This causes the joint to be unstable, in turn leading to arthritis and pain. Records registered with the Orthopedic Foundation for Animals (OFA) indicate that 11 percent of Cavaliers that had had their hips submitted for evaluation there are dysplastic. However, researchers believe this underestimates the true amount, which they believe may be as high as 33 percent.

Symptoms: Hip X-rays can detect hip dysplasia before outward signs are noticeable. In the United States, X-rays are usually rated by either the Orthopedic Foundation for Animals (OFA: *www.offa.org*) or the Pennsylvania Hip Improvement Program (PennHIP: *www.pennhip.org*).

Treatment: Mild cases may not need treatment, but in severe cases, the longer the condi-

tion persists, the more chance for arthritic changes to occur. In these cases, surgery is often the best choice.

Patellar luxation is the bane of many small breeds, including, to some extent, the Cavalier. In most dogs the patella (kneecap) is held in its proper position by a deep groove, but if the groove is too shallow (or if the tibia is misaligned) the patella can pop out of place. When out of place, the knee cannot be straightened and the dog will hold the leg up, usually only for a few steps at a time, but sometimes for extended periods. When standing, the leg may appear bowed either in or out.

Patellar luxation can be corrected surgically, the sooner the better. The longer the surgery is postponed, especially in a growing puppy, the greater the chance the leg will be permanently deformed. Patellar luxation is also discussed on pages 20 and 67.

Strange Behavior

Fly-catching behavior is considered to be a form of hallucinatory or epileptic behavior in which the dog snaps repeatedly in the air, as though trying to catch flying insects that are not there. It usually first appears between eight months and one and a half years of age. Consult your veterinarian if the episodes increase in frequency or magnitude. New treatments for epilepsy may be effective in controlling the behavior.

Symptoms of Common Health Problems

Coughing: Allergies, foreign bodies, pneumonia, parasites, tracheal collapse, tumors, and especially, kennel cough and heart disease, can all cause coughing.

Kennel cough is a highly communicable airborne disease caused by several different infectious agents. It is characterized by a gagging cough arising eight days after exposure. Inoculations are available and are an especially good idea if you plan to have your dog around other dogs at training classes or while being boarded.

Heart disease can result in coughing, most often following exercise or in the evening. See Mitral Valve Disease (page 68) for a description of this all too common problem of the Cavalier.

Any persistent cough should be checked by your veterinarian. Coughing irritates the throat and can lead to secondary infections if allowed to continue unchecked. It can also be miserable for the dog.

Vomiting

Vomiting is a common occurrence that may or may not indicate a serious problem. Vomiting after eating grass is common and usually of no great concern. Overeating is a common cause of occasional vomiting in puppies, especially if they follow eating with playing. Feed smaller meals more frequently if this becomes a problem. Vomiting immediately after meals could indicate an obstruction of the esophagus. Repeated vomiting could indicate that the dog has eaten spoiled food, undigestible objects, or may have stomach illness. Veterinary advice should be sought. Meanwhile withhold food (or feed as directed for diarrhea) and restrict water.

Consult your veterinarian immediately if your dog vomits a foul substance resembling fecal matter (indicating a blockage in the intestinal tract), blood (partially digested blood resembles coffee grounds), or if there is projectile or continued vomiting. Sporadic vomiting with poor appetite and generally poor condition could indicate internal parasites or a more serious internal disease that should also be checked by your veterinarian.

Diarrhea

Diarrhea can result from overexcitement or nervousness, a change in diet or water, sensitivity to certain foods, overeating, intestinal parasites, viral or bacterial infections, or ingestion of toxic substances. Bloody diarrhea, diarrhea with vomiting, fever, or other signs of toxicity, or a diarrhea that lasts for more than a day should not be allowed to continue without veterinary advice. Some of these symptoms could indicate potentially fatal disorders.

Less severe diarrhea can be treated at home by withholding or severely restricting food and water for 24 hours. Ice cubes can be given to satisfy thirst. Administer Pepto-Bismol in the same weight dosage as recommended for humans. A bland diet consisting of rice, tapioca, or cooked macaroni, along with cottage cheese or tofu for protein, should be given for several days. Feed nothing else. The intestinal tract needs time off in order to heal.

Urinary Tract Diseases

If your dog has difficulty or pain in urination, urinates suddenly and often but in small amounts, or passes cloudy or bloody urine, she may be suffering from a problem of the bladder, urethra, or (male) prostate. Dribbling of urine during sleep indicates a hormonal problem. Urinalysis and a rectal exam by your veterinarian are necessary to diagnose the exact nature of the problem. Bladder infections must be treated promptly to prevent the infection from reaching the kidneys.

Cavaliers, though generally healthy dogs, suffer from some hereditary medical conditions.

Kidney disease, ultimately leading to kidney failure, is one of the most common ailments of older dogs. The earliest symptom is usually increased urination. Although the excessive urination may cause problems in keeping your house clean or your night's sleep intact, *never* try to restrict water from a dog with kidney disease. Increased urination can also be a sign of diabetes or a urinary tract infection. Your veterinarian can discover the cause with some simple tests, and each of these conditions can be treated. For kidney disease, a low-protein and low-sodium diet can slow the progression.

In males, infections of the *prostate gland* can lead to repeated urinary tract infections, and sometimes painful defecation or blood and pus in the urine. Castration and long-term antibiotic therapy is required for improvement.

Impacted Anal Sacs

Constant licking of the anus or scooting of the anus along the ground are characteristic signs of anal sac impaction. Dogs have two anal sacs that are normally emptied by rectal pressure during defecation. Their musky-smelling contents may also be forcibly ejected when a dog is extremely frightened. Sometimes the sacs fail to empty properly and become impacted or infected. This is more common in small dogs, obese dogs, dogs with seborrhea, and dogs that seldom have firm stools. Impacted sacs cause extreme discomfort and can become infected. Treatment consists of manually emptying the sacs and administering antibiotics. As a last resort, the sacs may be removed surgically.

Endocrine Disorders

The most widespread hormone-related disorders in the dog are diabetes, hypothyroidism, and Cushing's syndrome.

• The most common of these, *hypothyroidism*, also has the least obvious symptoms, which may include weight gain, lethargy, and coat problems such as oiliness, dullness, *symmetrical* hair loss, and hair that is easily pulled out.

• The hallmark of *diabetes* is increased drinking and urination, and sometimes increased appetite with weight loss.

• *Cushing's syndrome* (hyperadrenocorticism) is seen mostly in older dogs, and is characterized by increased drinking and urination, potbellied appearance, symmetrical hair loss on the body, darkened skin, and susceptibility to infections.

All these conditions can be diagnosed with simple tests, and can be treated with drugs by your veterinarian.

Eye Problems

Those big brown eyes come with a price tag: their fairly large size makes them slightly more vulnerable to corneal scratches. Squinting or tearing can be due to an irritated cornea or foreign body. Examine under the lids and flood the eye with saline solution, or use a moist cotton swab to remove any debris. If no improvement is seen after a day, have your veterinarian take a look. A watery discharge without squinting can be a symptom of allergies or a tear drainage problem. A clogged tear drainage duct can cause the tears to drain onto the face, rather than the normal drainage through the nose. Your veterinarian can diagnose a drainage problem with a simple test.

KCS: A thick ropy mucous or crusty discharge suggests conjunctivitis or dry eye (*keratoconjunctivitis sicca*, or KCS). In KCS there is inadequate tear production, resulting in irritation to the surface of the eye whenever the dog blinks. The surface of the eye may appear dull. KCS can cause secondary bacterial infection or corneal ulcers. In fact, KCS should be suspected in any dog in which recurrent corneal ulceration or conjunctivitis is a problem. In past years KCS was treated with the frequent application of artificial tears, which most owners found difficult to dispense as often as needed. Recent drug advances treat the causes of KCS with ophthalmic immunosuppressive therapy. This therapy can be quite effective if begun early.

Cataracts: As your Cavalier ages it is natural that the lens of the eye becomes a little hazy. You will notice this as a slightly grayish appearance behind the pupils. But if this occurs at a young age, or if the lens looks white or opaque, ask your veterinarian to check your dog for *cataracts*. In cataracts the lens becomes so opaque that light can no longer reach the retina; as in humans, the lens can be surgically replaced with an artificial lens. Hereditary cataracts have been reported in Cavaliers.

Injury: If an eye is injured, cover it with clean gauze soaked in water or saline solution. For contact with irritants, flush for five minutes with water.

Any time your dog's pupils do not react to light or when one eye reacts differently from the other, consult the veterinarian immediately. These symptoms could indicate a serious ocular or neurological problem.

The eyes are such complex and sensitive organs that you should always err on the side of caution. Seek veterinary attention at the slightest sign of a problem.

Ear Care

The dog's ear canal is made up of an initial long vertical segment that then abruptly angles to run horizontally toward the skull. This configuration provides a moist environment in which various ear infections can flourish. Add to this the Cavalier's hanging ear flap, and you have the recipe for an ear problem, especially when the ears are covered with thick, heavy hair. At the same time, the Cavalier is not as prone to ear problems as are breeds in which the hair grows down into the ear canal. It is fairly simple to keep the Cavalier's ears healthy by checking them regularly and not allowing moisture or debris to build up in them.

Signs of problems: Signs of ear problems include inflammation, discharge, debris, foul odor, pain, scratching, shaking, tilting of the head, or circling to one side. Extreme pain may indicate a ruptured eardrum. Ear problems can be difficult to cure once they have become established, so early veterinary attention is crucial. Bacterial and fungal infections, ear mites or ticks, foreign bodies, inhalant allergies, seborrhea, or hypothyroidism are possible underlying problems. Grass awns are one of the most common causes of ear problems in dogs that spend time outdoors. Keep the ear lubricated with mineral oil, and seek veterinary treatment as soon as possible. Problems only get worse.

Treatment: When treating the ears with drops or liquids, you will have to wash the hair under the ear almost every day, or the oily liquid that is shaken from the ears will stick in the hair and can cause matting. Use a no-rinse shampoo and be careful not to get water or shampoo into the ear canal.

Don't stick cotton swabs into the ear canal; they can irritate the skin and pack debris into the horizontal canal. Never use powders in the ear, which can cake, or hydrogen peroxide, which leaves the ear moist.

Ear mites: Ear mites, often found in puppies, are highly contagious and intensely irritating. An affected dog will shake its head, scratch its ears, and carry its head sideways. A dark, dry, waxy buildup resembling coffee grounds, usually in the ear canal of both ears, is the ear mite's signature. This material is actually dried blood mixed with ear wax. Over-the-counter ear mite preparations can cause worse irritation; ear mites are best treated by your veterinarian.

Many people automatically assume any ear problem is due to ear mites, but unless you actually see mites, don't treat the dog for them. You could make another problem worse.

The smelly dog: Doggy odor is not only offensive; it is unnatural. Don't exile the dog, or hold your breath. If a bath doesn't produce results, it's time to use your nose to sniff out the source of the problem. Infection is a common cause of bad odor; check the mouth, ears, feet, and genitals. Generalized bad odor can indicate a skin problem, such as seborrhea. Don't ignore bad odor, and don't make your dog take the blame for something you need to fix.

To a Ripe Old Age

The Cavalier's perpetual puppy persona and look sometimes mislead owners into forgetting that Cavaliers, like all dogs, get old. One day you will look at your Cavalier and be shocked to discover her face has silvered and her gait has stiffened. She sleeps longer and more soundly than she did as a youngster, and is slower to get going. She may be less eager to play and more content to lie in the sun. Though you might feel sad, be mindful that getting your dog to healthy old age is a worthy accomplishment. Just make sure that you appreciate all the stages along the way.

Cavalier Golden Years

Cavaliers have an average life span of 9 to 14 years, with many living well into their teens. As with people, some are simply genetically destined to live shorter lives than others, and some are the victims of accidents. But you can do your part to supply the best of care that will ensure that your Cavalier can live the fullest and longest life she can.

Exercise: Older Cavaliers are among the most gracious of elders, but they often retain that

———— TIP ————

The Tribute

One of the noblest tributes to a cherished Cavalier is to make a donation to a canine welfare organization such as a Cavalier rescue group or health research project (see page 93).

puppy dog aura that belies their years. They still need lots of mental and physical stimulation, but not at the level they did as youngsters. With advancing age, you may need to take extra precautions against stress, overheating, chilling, and injuries. That may mean spending more time playing indoor games that aren't too physically demanding, or simply sharing time riding in the car, assisting with the laundry, planning the menu, or walking around the block.

Arthritis slows many older dogs. Keeping weight down, providing a warm, soft bed, attending to injuries, and maintaining a program of low-impact exercise can help mild cases. Drugs and supplements can also help. Polysulfated glycosaminoglycan increases the compressive resilience of cartilage; glucosamine stimulates collagen synthesis and may help rejuvenate cartilage; and chondroitin sulfate helps shield cartilage from destructive enzymes. Anti-inflammatory drugs may help alleviate some pain, but must be used with veterinary supervision.

Feeding: Keeping an older Cavalier svelte can be a challenge, but it's important. Excessive weight places an added burden on the heart, back, and joints. Most healthy older Cavs

don't need a special diet, but they should receive high-quality protein. When dogs get extremely old, they tend to lose weight, and at some point keeping adequate weight on them may be a challenge. Adding canned food, cooked meat or other treats can help older dogs enjoy their meals.

Behavioral changes: Many older dogs suffer from cognitive dysfunction, in which they appear confused, depressed, or disoriented. Challenging their minds with games or new tricks every day can help stave it off. Your veterinarian can also prescribe drug therapy that may give good results.

What you may attribute to senility may just be loss of hearing with age. Your Cavalier's vision and hearing may fade, so be sure she can't wander off where she can't see or hear you. Dogs with hearing loss can learn to respond to hand signals, vibrating collars, and flashing lights using the same training techniques you used to teach voice commands. Dogs with vision loss can cope well as long as you keep them in familiar surroundings, place sound or scent beacons at key locations, and block off pools and steps.

Tooth, nail, and skin care: Don't ignore stronger body odors, which can signal periodontal disease, impacted anal sacs, seborrhea, or ear infections. Regular brushing can help soothe dry, itchy skin by stimulating oil production. The nails tend to get especially long in older dogs, so you'll need to cut them more often.

Now is the time to address any dental problems. Bad breath, lip licking, reluctance to chew, or swelling around the mouth can all signal periodontal disease. A thorough tooth cleaning and perhaps drug therapy is needed.

Health: A senior Cavalier should have a checkup twice a year. That's not excessive when you consider the rate at which they are aging. Tests can detect early stages of treatable diseases.

Older dogs may have less efficient immune systems, making it more important to shield them from infectious diseases or stress. However, if your dog stays home all the time, she may not need to be vaccinated as often as when she was younger; this is an area of controversy that you should discuss with your veterinarian.

Dogs suffer from many of the same diseases of old age that humans do.

• Cancer accounts for almost half the deaths of dogs over the age of 10 years. Its signs include weight or appetite loss, collapse, swellings, lameness, difficulty swallowing, or lethargy, among others.

• Heart disease, often signaled by weakness, coughing, or fluid accumulation in the tissues of the limbs or belly, is also a major problem of older dogs.

• Kidney disease, signaled by increased thirst and urination, is yet another major problem.

• Cushing's Syndrome (hyperadrenocorticism) is also seen more often in older dogs. Its signs include increased hunger, thirst, and urination, as well as hair loss, muscle atrophy, and a pot belly.

Farewell to a Friend

After losing such a cherished friend, many people say they will never get another dog. True, no dog will ever take the place of your dog. But you will find that another Cavalier is a welcome diversion and will help keep you from dwelling on the loss of your first pet, as long as you don't keep comparing the new dog to the old. True also, by getting another dog you are sentencing yourself to the same grief one day, but wouldn't you rather have that than miss out on a second once-in-a-lifetime dog?

For the following situations, initiate first aid and then transport to the veterinarian (call first).

Shock

Signs: Weakness, collapse, pale gums, unresponsiveness, and faint pulse.

Treatment: Since it may occur in almost any case of trauma, it's usually best to treat the dog as though she were in shock. Keep her warm and quiet, and keep her head low compared to her heart (unless she has a head wound).

Heatstroke

Signs: Initially, rapid loud breathing, abundant thick saliva, bright red mucous membranes, and high rectal temperature. Later, unsteadiness, diarrhea, and coma.

Treatment: Wet the dog down and place her in front of a fan. If this isn't possible, immerse her in cold water. Don't plunge her in ice water, because that constricts the peripheral blood vessels so much that it actually traps the hot blood in the core of the body, doing more damage. Offer water to drink.

You must lower your dog's body temperature, but don't let the temperature go below 100°F (37.8°C). Stop cooling when the rectal temperature reaches 103°F (39.4°C) because it will continue to fall.

Even when the temperature is back to normal your dog is still in danger and still needs veterinary attention. It will take several days for your dog to recover, during which she should not exert herself.

Breathing Difficulties

Signs: gasping for breath with head extended, anxiety, weakness; advances to unconsciousness, bluish tongue (Exception: carbon monoxide poisoning causes bright red tongue.)

Treatment: If not breathing:

1. Open dog's mouth, clear passage of secretions and foreign bodies.

2. Pull dog's tongue forward.

3. Seal your mouth over dog's nose and mouth, blow gently into dog's nose for three seconds, then release.

4. Continue until dog breathes on her own.

Note: In case of **drowning**, turn dog upside down, holding around her waist, so water can run out of her mouth. Then administer mouth-to-nose respiration, with the dog's head positioned lower than her lungs.

For obstructions, wrap your hands around the abdomen, behind the rib cage, and compress briskly. Repeat if needed. If the dog loses consciousness, extend the head and neck forward, pull the tongue out fully, and explore the throat for any foreign objects.

Hypothermia

Signs: Shivering, cold feeling, sluggishness.

Cool an overheated dog by covering it with wet towels and placing it in front of a fan.

Treatment: Warm gradually. Wrap in blanket. Place plastic bottles filled with hot water outside the blankets (not touching the dog). You can also place a plastic tarp over the blanket, making sure the dog's head is not covered. Monitor temperature.

Convulsions or Seizures
Signs: drooling, stiffness, muscle spasms
Treatment: Wrap the dog securely in a blanket to prevent her from injuring herself on furniture or stairs. Remove other dogs from the area (they may attack the convulsing dog). Never put your hands (or anything) in a convulsing dog's mouth. Treat for shock. Make note of all characteristics and sequences of seizure to help diagnose the cause.

Hypoglycemia (low blood sugar)
Signs: Appears disoriented, weak, staggering. May appear blind, and muscles may twitch. Later stages lead to convulsions, coma, and death.
Treatment: Give food, or honey or syrup mixed with warm water.

Open Wounds
Signs: Wounds are an emergency if there is profuse bleeding, if extremely deep, if open to chest cavity, abdominal cavity, or head.
Treatment: Control massive bleeding first. Cover the wound with clean dressing and apply pressure; apply more dressings over the others until bleeding stops. Also elevate wound site, and apply cold pack to site. If an extremity, apply pressure to the closest pressure point as follows:
- For a front leg: inside of front leg just above the elbow
- For a rear leg: inside of thigh where the femoral artery crosses the thigh-bone

Apply pressure to the closest pressure point for uncontrolled bleeding of an extremity.

- For the tail: underside of tail close to where it joins the body.

Use a tourniquet only in life-threatening situations and when all other attempts have failed. Check for signs of shock.

Sucking Chest Wounds
Place plastic or other nonporous sheet over the hole and bandage it to make an airtight seal.

Abdominal Wounds
Place warm wet sterile dressing over any protruding internal organs; cover with bandage or towel. Do not attempt to push organs back.

Head Wounds
Apply gentle pressure to control bleeding. Monitor for loss of consciousness or shock and treat accordingly.

THE CAVALIER COMPETITOR

As much pleasure as your Cavalier gives you just being your best friend at home, don't ignore the great times awaiting both of you elsewhere. Between beauty contests, mind games, therapy work, and outdoor adventures, you just may find yourself busier than ever.

Cavalcade of Cavaliers

Cavaliers and their Toy Spaniel ancestors have been a steady presence in the show rings of England since the turn of the twentieth century. In fact, it could be said that the Cavalier King Charles Spaniel was born at a dog show, since it was Roswell Eldridge's challenge in the form of a class prize offered at the Crufts show in 1926 that planted the seed for the breed. Crufts is one of the largest and most prestigious shows in the world, and so perhaps it was only fitting that in the 1973 show the fruits of that seed, in the form of Ch Alansmere Aquarius, was judged Best in Show at Crufts over thousands of dogs representing over 100 other breeds. Perhaps one day soon Crufts' American counterpart, the Westminster Dog Show, will be conquered by another Englander.

Even in the United States, the Cavalier is no newcomer to dog shows. The CKCSC, USA has held its own shows and awarded its own championships for decades. With entries sometimes numbering in the hundreds, winning any award at these events is no small feat. The result of the importation of dogs from top English lines, combined with the tough competition among American dogs, has resulted in a breed that is poised to compete at the highest caliber of competition.

The AKC Standard

General Appearance

The Cavalier King Charles Spaniel is an active, graceful, well-balanced toy spaniel, very gay and free in action; fearless and sporting in character, yet at the same time gentle and affectionate. It is this typical gay temperament, combined with true elegance and royal appearance, which are of paramount importance to the breed. Natural appearance with no trimming, sculpting, or artificial alteration is essential to breed type.

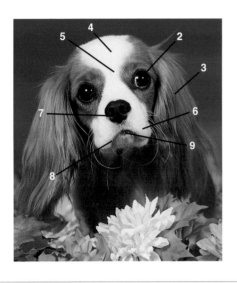

1 Expression is sweet, gentle, and melting.
2 Eyes are large, round, but not prominent; set well apart. Dark brown in color, with dark rims. Cushioning under eye.
3 Ears are set high, with long leather and lots of feathering.
4 Skull is slightly rounded, but without dome or peak.
5 Stop is moderate, neither filled nor deep.
6 Muzzle is full, slightly tapered. Length from base of stop to tip of nose about 1½ inches [3.8 cm].
7 Nose is uniformly black, with well developed nostrils.
8 Lips are well developed but not pendulous.
9 Bite is scissors.

Size, Proportion, Substance

Size: Height 12 to 13 inches [31–33 cm] at the withers; weight proportionate to height, between 13 and 18 lbs. [6–8 kg]. A small, well-balanced dog within these weights is desirable, but these are ideal heights and weights and slight variations are permissible.

Proportion: The body approaches squareness, yet if measured from point of shoulder to point of buttock, is slightly longer than the height at the withers. The height from the withers to the elbow is approximately equal to the height from the elbow to the ground.

Substance: Bone moderate in proportion to size. Weedy and coarse specimens are to be equally penalized.

Coat: Of moderate length, silky, free from curl. Slight wave permissible. Feathering on ears, chest, legs, and tail should be long, and the feathering on the feet is a feature of the breed. No trimming of the dog is permitted. *Specimens where the coat has been altered by trimming, clipping, or by artificial means shall be so severely penalized as to be effectively eliminated from competition.* Hair growing between the pads on the underside of the feet may be trimmed.

Color: *Blenheim*—Rich chestnut markings well broken up on a clear, pearly white ground. The ears must be chestnut and the color evenly spaced on the head and surrounding both eyes, with a white blaze between the eyes and ears, in the center of which may be the lozenge or "Blenheim spot." The lozenge is a unique and desirable, though not essential, characteristic of the Blenheim. *Tricolor*—Jet black markings well broken up on a clear, pearly white ground. The ears must be black and the color evenly spaced on the head and surrounding both eyes, with a white blaze between the eyes. Rich tan markings over the eyes, on cheeks, inside ears, and

Points of the Cavalier Standard

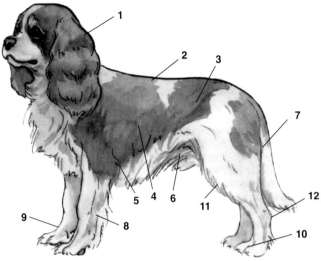

1. Neck is fairly long, without throatiness. It forms a slight arch at the crest, and flows smoothly into shoulders.
2. Topline is level when moving or standing.
3. Body is short-coupled.
4. Ribs are well-sprung but not barreled.
5. Chest is moderately deep, extending to elbows.
6. No appearance of tuck-up, although there is slightly less body at the flank than at the last rib.

7. Tail is carried happily but never much above the level of the back. It is in constant motion when the dog is in action.
8. Forelegs are straight and well under dog, with elbows close to the side.
9. Pasterns are strong.
10. Feet are compact with well-cushioned pads.
11. Stifles are well turned.
12. Hocks are low.

on underside of tail. *Ruby*—Whole-colored rich red. *Black and Tan*—Jet black with rich, bright tan markings over the eyes, on cheeks, inside ears, on chest, legs, and on underside of tail. *Faults*—Heavy ticking on Blenheims and Tricolors, white marks on Rubies or Black and Tans.

Gait: Free-moving and elegant in action, with good reach in front and sound, driving rear action. When viewed from the side, the movement exhibits a good length of stride, and viewed from front and rear it is straight and true, resulting from straight-boned fronts and properly made and muscled hindquarters.

Temperament: Gay, friendly, non-aggressive with no tendency toward nervousness or shyness. *Bad temper, shyness, and meanness are not to be tolerated and are to be so severely penalized as to effectively remove the specimen from competition.*

Mind Games

If your Cavalier is more than just a pretty face, you may wish to show off his brain power and earn a Canine Good Citizen, rally, or obedience title.

The Cavalier Good Citizen

The Canine Good Citizen (CGC) certificate attests that your dog is well-behaved in public. To show what a good citizen he is he will have to:

✔ Accept a friendly stranger without acting shy or resentful, or breaking position to approach; sitting politely for petting and allowing the stranger to examine his ears, feet, and coat, and to brush him.

✔ Walk politely on a loose leash, turning and stopping with you, walking through a group of at least three other people without jumping on them, pulling, or acting overly exuberant, shy, or resentful. She need not be perfectly aligned with you, but she shouldn't be pulling.

✔ *Sit* and *lie* down on command (you can gently guide him into position) and the *stay* as you walk 20 feet (51 cm) away and back.

✔ *Stay* and then come to you when called from 10 feet (25 cm) away.

✔ Behave politely to another dog and handler team, showing only casual interest in them.

✔ React calmly to distractions such as a dropped chair or passing jogger without panicking, barking, or acting aggressively.

✔ Remain calm when held by a stranger while you're out of sight for three minutes.

✔ Refrain from eliminating, growling, snapping, biting, or attempting to attack a person or dog throughout the evaluation.

Bring his buckle or slip collar, brush or comb, and proof of rabies vaccination.

All the tests are done on lead; a long line is provided for the Stay and Recall exercises. If your Cavalier passes, he will receive a Canine Good Citizen certificate from the AKC.

The expression is sweet, gentle, and melting.

Rally

Rally obedience is just one step above the CGC in difficulty. It's an easy going style of obedience in which you and your dog follow a course along which various signs telling you what to do next are placed. Directions include things such as *Sit*, *Step to the side*, *Spiral*, and *Jump*. Three levels are offered: novice, advanced, and excellent, leading to the Rally Novice (RN), Rally Advanced (RA), and Rally Excellent (RE) titles. The novice levels are all done on leash, but the other levels are performed off leash. You can praise and talk to your dog throughout, and repeat commands. The dog's willingness and enjoyment are more important than is precision.

Obedience

You plan on training your Cavalier the commands *Heel*, *Sit*, *Down*, *Come*, and *Stay* for use in everyday life. Add the *Stand for Exam*, and your dog will have the basic skills necessary to earn the AKC Companion Dog (CD) title.

Higher degrees of Companion Dog Excellent (CDX), Utility Dog (UD), Utility Dog Excellent (UDX), and Obedience Trial Champion (OTCH) also may require retrieving, jumping, hand signals, and scent discrimination.

Hot on the Trail

Some dogs have a more innate tendency to trail, but all breeds can be taught to use their noses and track. A Tracking Dog (TD) title is earned by following a human trail about 500 yards (153 m) long that was laid up to two hours earlier. More advanced titles of Tracking Dog Excellent (TDX) and Variable Surface Tracker (VST) can also be earned.

Agility

Agility is basically an obstacle course for dogs. The standard AKC course obstacles include various jumps, open and closed tunnels, weave poles, a pause table, a teeter, a tall A-frame, and an elevated balance beam. The jumps can be single bars, double bars, broad, solid, and even a tire. An alternative course type, called Jumpers With Weaves (JWW) just uses the jumps, tunnels, and weaves. If the jumps seem too high for your dog you can elect to compete in the Preferred class, which has lower jump heights. All of the classes have Novice, Open, and Excellent levels with progressively harder courses and shorter times. Your job is to guide your dog from obstacle to obstacle off lead within a certain time limit. Your dog must pass at each level three times to earn each agility title.

Don't stop there! The world of canine competition has something for everyone! How about freestyle, where dogs and their people dance to music, or flyball, where dogs compete on relay teams to run down a short course with four low jumps, catch a ball, and return?

TIP

CKCSC, USA Events

The CKCSC, USA has been holding competitions and awarding titles to Cavaliers longer than any other organization in America. They award conformation, obedience, agility, and tracking titles, as well as children's handling competitions. For more information and a list of upcoming events go to *www.ckcsc.org*.

THE CAVALIER COMPANION

Cavaliers and their owners tend to share an almost uncanny bond, as well as an eagerness to share all aspects of their lives. Although snuggling in front of the hearth may be sufficient for some people and their dogs, others will want to include their dogs on greater adventures.

The Gypsy King

Whether you are journeying around the country or around the block, you and your Cavalier will be held up to scrutiny by people who have seen too many ill-mannered dogs. For the sake of dog ownership in the future, maintain the highest public standards:

✔ Always clean up after your dog. Carry a little plastic bag for disposal later.

✔ Don't let your dog run loose where it could bother picnickers, bicyclists, joggers, or children.

✔ Never let your dog bark unchecked.

✔ Never let your dog jump up on people.

✔ Never take a chance of your dog's biting anybody.

Cavaliers make excellent travel companions. They are small enough to fit handily into any car, yet large enough to share most outdoor adventures along the way. A dog gives you a good excuse to stop and enjoy the scenery up close, and maybe even get some exercise along the way. With proper planning, you will find that a Cavalier companion can make your trip even better.

Do's and Don'ts While Traveling

1. Without proper planning, sharing your trip with any dog can be a nightmare, as you are turned away from motels, parks, and beaches. It's no fun sleeping in your car, or trying to sneak a dog past the front desk of a motel. Several books are available listing establishments that accept pets. Call ahead to attractions to see if they have arrangements for pets.

2. Whether you will be spending your nights at a motel, campground, or even a friend's home, always have your dog on her very best behavior. Ask beforehand if it will be OK for you to bring your Cavalier. Have your dog clean and parasite-free. Do not allow your dog to run helter-skelter through the homes of friends. Bring your dog's own clean blanket or bed, or

better yet, her crate. Your Cav will appreciate the familiar place to sleep, and your friends and motel owners will breathe sighs of relief. Even though your dog may be accustomed to sleeping on furniture at home, a proper canine guest stays on the floor when visiting.

3. Walk and walk your dog (and clean up after her) to make sure no accidents occur inside. If they do, clean them immediately. Don't leave any surprises for your hosts! Changes in water or food, or simply stress can often result in diarrhea, so be particularly attentive to taking your dog out often.

4. Never, never leave your dog unattended in a strange place. The dog's perception is that you have left and forgotten her; she either barks or tries to dig her way out through the doors and windows in an effort to find you, or becomes upset and relieves herself on the carpet. Always remember that anyone who allows your dog to spend the night is doing so with a certain amount of trepidation; make sure your Cavalier is so well behaved that they invite both of you back.

5. Always walk your Cavalier on lead when away from home. If frightened or distracted, your dog could become disoriented and lost. The long retractable leads are excellent for traveling. Keep an eye out for little nature excursions, which are wonderful for refreshing both dog and owner. But always do so with a cautious eye; never risk your own or your dog's safety by stopping in totally desolate locales, no matter how breathtaking the view.

6. While in the car your Cavalier will want to cuddle in your lap or close by your side, or hang her head out the window for a big whiff of country air. You are smarter than your Cavalier, however, and know that it should always ride with the equivalent of a doggy seat belt:

Items for Your Cavalier's Own Travel Case

- first aid kit
- heartworm preventive and any other medications, especially antidiarrhea medication
- food and water bowls
- dog biscuits and chewies
- flea spray
- flea comb and brush
- bedding
- short and long leashes
- sweater for cold weather
- flashlight for night walks
- plastic baggies or other poop disposal means
- moist towelettes, paper towels, and self-rinse shampoo
- food
- bottled water or water from home—many dogs are very sensitive to changes in water and can develop diarrhea
- license tags, including a tag indicating where you could be reached while on your trip, or including the address of someone you know will be at home
- health and rabies certificates
- recent color photo in case your Cav somehow gets lost

the crate. Not only can a crate help prevent accidents by keeping your dog from using your lap as a trampoline, but if an accident does happen a crate can save your dog's life. A crate with a padlocked door can also be useful when you need to leave the dog in the car with the windows down.

With a little foresight you may find your Cavalier King Charles Spaniel to be the most entertaining and enjoyable travel companion you could invite along. And don't be surprised if you find your dog nestled in your suitcase among your packed clothes!

Boarding

Sometimes you must leave your dog behind when you travel. Ask friends or your veterinarian for boarding kennel recommendations. The ideal kennel will be approved by the American Boarding Kennel Association, have climate-controlled accommodations, and will keep your Cavalier either indoors or in a combination indoor/outdoor run. Make an unannounced visit to the kennel and ask to see the facilities. While you can't expect spotlessness and a perfumed atmosphere, most runs should be clean and the odor should not be overpowering. All dogs should have clean water and at least some dogs should have soft bedding. Good kennels will require proof of immunizations, and an incoming check for fleas. They will allow you to bring toys and bedding, and will administer prescribed medication. Strange dogs should not be allowed to mingle, and the entire kennel area should be fenced.

Your dog may be more comfortable if an experienced pet sitter or responsible friend comes to your home and feeds and exercises your dog regularly. This works best if you have a doggy door. The kid next door is seldom a good choice for this important responsibility. It is too easy for the dog to slip out the door, or for signs of illness to go unnoticed, unless the sitter is an experienced dog person. The life of your dog is a heavy responsibility for a child. A bonded pet sitter may cost a little more, but is well worth the extra peace of mind.

Important: Whatever means you choose, always leave emergency numbers and your vet-

erinarian's name. Make arrangements with your veterinarian to treat your dog for any problems that may arise. This means leaving a written agreement stating that you give permission for treatment and accept responsibility for charges.

Destinations

Ready to get out of the house but don't know where your dog is welcome? Consider organizing a play group with your friends, neighbors, or fellow members of your training or conformation club. Find an outdoor café and do lunch together. Volunteer at a meet and greet, an event in which dogs of various breeds meet the public. Arrange a charity event, perhaps a doggy carnival or other doggy event. Dog parks are the in thing in many cities, and they can be great places for dogs to play together and run in a safely enclosed area. But your Cavalier is smaller than most dogs, and it's not a good idea to let her run with a group of large dogs, no matter how friendly. It takes only an inadvertent bump, especially if the excitement level is already high, for several dogs to pile on a little dog.

If you do travel farther afield in search of adventure, plan ahead. Many big city hotels cater to canine clientele, and even some resort motels offer special hospitality to canine guests. You can go to a dog-friendly beach, a dude ranch, or even on a dog paddling canoe adventure.

How about camp? Unlike children's camps, you get to go too! Your Cavalier can try out all sorts of dog sports, go hiking and swimming, or just lounge around and be sociable. Some camps specialize in certain skills whereas others just specialize in fun.

Take a Hike!

Cavaliers can entertain themselves quite ably within the confines of your own yard, but they will jump at the chance for an adventure afield. Regular exercise is the cure for many behavioral problems, especially in younger dogs.

Cavaliers make wonderful short-distance hiking companions, but their Spaniel heritage will sometimes lead them astray unless you keep an eye on them. Bringing along another reliable dog that stays with you is the best training aid you can have.

Everybody thinks their dog is smart and trustworthy and reliable off lead. They are usually right—until the unpredictable occurs: another dog attacks, or a cat runs underfoot. Whatever the reason, the trustworthy dog forgets itself for just a moment—and that's all it takes to run in front of a car. Trust is wonderful, but careless or blind trust is deadly.

In many areas there simply are no safe places in which to run your Cavalier off lead. Your dog can get ample exercise and enjoyment from a walk on lead. Before walking on lead, double check that your dog's collar cannot slip over her head. A startled dog can frantically back out of its collar unless it is snug. If you use a retractable leash, never allow so much loose lead that your dog could suddenly jump into the path of a passing vehicle.

Check your dog's foot pads regularly for signs of abrasion, foreign bodies, tears, or blistering from hot pavement. Leave your dog at home in hot weather. Dogs are unable to cool themselves through sweating, and heatstroke in jogging dogs is a common emergency seen by veterinarians in the summer. In winter, check between the foot pads for balls of ice (clipping the long hair between the pads and coating the paws with Vaseline can help keep the ice balls down somewhat) and rinse the feet when returning from walking on rock salt. If you pick a regular time of day for your walk you will have your own personal fitness coach goading you off the couch like clockwork.

Swimming is an excellent exercise, especially in the summer or for dogs with arthritis or other injuries. Most Cavaliers take right to the water, but if you have one that needs a little coaxing, get right into the water with her and ease her gradually in. Support its rear end so that it doesn't splash on top of the water, and you will soon have a little otter on your hands.

Little Dog Lost

Cavaliers have a tendency to go where the wind blows them. When they quit sniffing flowers and chasing butterflies, they look up

and suddenly realize they don't know where they are. Of course you must never allow your Cav to find herself in such a situation, but if your dog does wander off, you need to act quickly. Don't rely on the dog's fabled ability to find her way home. You hear only about the few who make it. Too many dogs seem to have no sense of direction.

Start your search at the very worst place you could imagine your dog going, usually the nearest highway. Don't drive recklessly and endanger your own dog's life should she run across the road. If you still can't find your pet, get pictures of her and go door to door; ask any workers or delivery persons in the area. Call the local animal control, police department, and veterinarians. If your dog is tattooed or microchipped, contact the registry. Make up large posters with a picture of your dog or a similar-looking Cavalier. Take out an ad in the local paper. Mention a reward, but do not specify an amount.

As Cavaliers continue to gain public attention they will become increasingly attractive to dognappers. Never leave your dog in a place where she could be taken. Never give anyone reward money before seeing your dog. There are a

to be read. You may wish to discuss this option with your veterinarian or local breeders.

The Comforter Spaniel

Cavaliers excel at many roles, but it is no surprise that their forte is the role of companion par excellence. The Cavalier's first claim to fame was as a "comforter spaniel," bred to bring both physical and emotional comfort to those whose lives it graced. Today the role of the comforter spaniel is as vital as ever.

Studies have shown that pet ownership increases life expectancy and petting animals can lower blood pressure. You know how your Cavalier picks up your spirits when you're down. Have you considered sharing her antics and affection with somebody who has no access to a dog? It could be a visit to a shut-in neighbor, a nursing home resident, or a hospitalized child. You could educate schoolchildren on dog care or entertain challenged children. Cavaliers are among the most talented therapy dogs, seeming to know just the right thing to do whether visiting children or adults, and whether they are for sick, mentally, physically, or emotionally challenged.

To become an official therapy dog, you'll need to get some instruction and your dog will need to demonstrate that she's gentle, well-mannered, and tolerant of what can sometimes become heavy petting. Of course she'll need to be clean before visiting! Most larger cities have training programs so your dog can become a recognized therapy dog. They will also train you so you know how to handle yourself and your dog in various situations. Sharing your Cavalier is one of the most rewarding activities the two of you can pursue. The loving Cavalier is still comforting after all these years.

number of scams involving answering lost dog ads, many asking for money for shipping the dog back to you from a distance or for paying veterinarian's bills, when very often these people have not really found your dog. If your dog is tattooed, you can have the person read the tattoo to you in order to positively identify her.

Even license tags cannot always ensure your dog's return, because they must be on the dog to be effective. Tattooing your social security number or your dog's registration number on the inside of her thigh provides a permanent means of identification; these numbers can be registered with one of the several lost pet recovery agencies. Microchips are available that are placed under the dog's skin with a simple injection. They contain information about the dog and cannot be removed, but require a special scanner (owned by most animal shelters)

INFORMATION

Clubs

American Cavalier King Charles Spaniel Club:
   www.ackcsc.org
Cavalier King Charles Spaniel Club (UK):
   www.thecavalierclub.co.uk
Cavalier King Charles Spaniel Club-USA:
   www.ckcsc.org
Cavalier King Charles Spaniel Club of Canada:
   www.cavaliercanada.com
American Kennel Club:
   www.akc.org

Internet Sites

Animal Poison Control Center:
   (888) 426-4435
   www.aspca.org
Cavalier Health:
   www.cavalierhealth.org
Cavalier Infocenter:
   www.premiercavalierinfosite.com
Cavalier Talk Board:
   www.cavaliertalk.com
Cavalier Web:
   http://cavalierkingcharles.org.uk/
Cavaliers Online:
   www.cavaliersonline.com
Cavaliers UK:
   www.cavaliers.co.uk
CKCS Magazine on the Net:
   www.ckcs.se
Cavalier books:
   www.dogwise.com

Magazines

The Royal Dispatch:
   www.ackcsc.org/royaldispatch.htm
The Royal Spaniels Magazine:
   www.the-royal-spaniels.com
Universal Cavalier Internet Magazine:
   www.universalcavalier.com
Top Notch Toys: *www.dmcg.com/pubs/*
   topnotchtoys/tnt_index.html

Health Research Foundations

ACKCSC Charitable Trust:
   www.ackcsccharitabletrust.org
Cavalier Health Foundation:
   www.cavalierhealthfoundation.com
Canine Health Foundation:
   www.akcchf.org
Morris Animal Foundation:
   www.morrisanimalfoundation.org

Health Registries

CKCSUSA Health Registry:
   http://www.ckcsc.org/ckcsc/healthreg.nsf/
   obn!openform
Canine Eye Registration Foundation:
   www.vmdb.org/cerf.html
Orthopedic Foundation for Animals:
   www.offa.org
Canine Health Information Center:
   www.caninehealthinfo.org

Rescue Groups

Cavalier Rescue USA:
   www.cavalierrescueusa.org
ACKCSC Rescue:
   www.ackcsc.org/rescue.htm
Lucky Star Cavalier Rescue:
   www.luckystarcavalierrescue.org
Pet Finder:
   www.petfinder.com
CKCS Canada Rescue:
   http://cavaliercanada.com/content/view/36/87
Cavalier Rescue UK:
   www.cavalierrescue.co.uk
Cavaliers of the South:
   www.cne-ckcsc.org/rescue.html
Cavaliers of the Northeast:
   www.cne-ckcsc.org/rescue.html
Cavaliers of the Midwest:
   www.cmw-ckcsc.org/cmwrescue.htm
Cavaliers of the West:
   www.cavaliersofthewest.org/rescue.htm

INDEX

About the Author

Caroline Coile is an award-winning author who has written thirty books about dogs, as well as hundreds of articles. She has been an active dog fancier and student of dogs for more than thirty years.

Acknowledgments

The author is indebted to members of the CKCS-L list for their many, sometimes overwhelming, but always valuable contributions to the text. I truly believe that this is one of the most knowledgeable and helpful groups of dog fanciers to be found on the Internet.

Important Note

This pet owner's manual tells the reader how to buy or adopt and care for a Cavalier King Charles Spaniel. The author and publisher consider it important to point out that the advice given in this book is meant primarily for normally developed dogs of excellent physical health and good character.

Anyone who adopts a fully grown dog should be aware that the animal has already formed its basic impressions of humans. The new owner should watch the dog carefully, including its behavior toward humans, and should meet the previous owner.

Caution is further advised in the association of children with dogs, in meeting with other dogs, and in exercising the dog without proper safeguards.

Even well-behaved and carefully supervised dogs sometimes do damage to someone else's property or cause accidents. It is therefore in the owner's interest to be adequately insured against such eventualities, and we strongly urge all dog owners to purchase a liability policy that covers their dog(s).

Cover Photos

Front cover: Isabelle Francais; back cover: Norvia Behling; inside front cover spread and inside back cover spread: Kent Dannen.

Photo Credits

Norvia Behling: 12, 16, 27, 29, 30, 36, 45, 46, 51, 58, 81, and 86; Kent Dannen: 24, 44, and 87; Isabelle Francais: 2–3, 4, 5, 7, 8, 15, 18, 20, 23, 25, 26, 37, 38, 40, 41, 47, 48, 52, 55, 64, 69, 73, 77, 80, 84, 89, 91, and 92; Pets by Paulette: 11, 13, 14, 50, and 82; and Connie Summers: 35, 39, and 59.

© Copyright 2008, 1998 by D. Caroline Coile.

All inquiries should be addressed to:
Barron's Educational Series, Inc.
250 Wireless Boulevard
Hauppauge, NY 11788
www.barronseduc.com

ISBN-13: 978-0-7641-3771-6
ISBN-10: 0-7641-3771-9

Library of Congress Catalog Card No. 2008009060

Library of Congress Cataloging-in-Publication Data
Coile, D. Caroline.
    Cavalier King Charles spaniels : everything about purchase, care, nutrition, behavior, and training / D. Caroline Coile ; full-color photographs ; illustrations by Michele Earle-Bridges.
        p. cm.
    Includes bibliographical references and index.
    ISBN-13: 978-0-7641-3771-6
    ISBN-10: 0-7641-3771-9
    1. Cavalier King Charles spaniel. I. Title.

SF429.C36C65 2008
636.752'4—dc22   2008009060

Printed in China
9 8 7 6